Fundraising for
Early Childhood Programs:
Getting Started and Getting Results

Fundraising for Early Childhood Programs: Getting Started and Getting Results

Matia Finn
The Bush Center in Child Development and
Social Policy—Yale University

National Association for the Education of
Young Children—Washington, D.C.

Book design: Melanie Rose White

The National Association for the Education of Young Children attempts through its publications program to provide a forum for discussion of major issues and ideas in our field. We hope to provoke thought and promote professional growth. The views expressed or implied are not necessarily those of the Association.

Library of Congress Catalog Card Number: 82-61245
ISBN Catalog Number: 0-912674-81-4
NAEYC #120

Printed in the United States of America.

Contents

Foreword

The new environment of private fundraising created by reductions in government funding does not affect all nonprofit, charitable organizations equally. Readers of this book, as advocates for children's causes, should realize that they are generally in a highly preferred category as compared with many other seekers of philanthropic funds.

This is because donors, by and large, want their funds to accomplish as much good as possible. Most donors are positive-minded and optimistic. The idea that the proper influences upon children can achieve much more than expensive, remedial programs later on is a very powerful incentive.

Of course this broad factor in your favor is only as useful as the specific efforts you bring to enlisting support for your cause. In fundraising, as in so many other activities, you can never just rely on your advantages. You must actively implement them in your work. For such an implementation to be successful, Matia Finn's wise, thorough, understandable, up-to-date, and realistic explanation of fundraising is a top-quality aid.

Henry C. Suhrke
Editor
Philanthropy Monthly

Preface

The nonprofit sector in America is a major employer and growth industry. Philanthropic organizations employ more than 5 million people, or approximately 14 percent of all professionals and 15 percent of all service workers. The philanthropic payroll exceeds $7.5 billion and the nonprofit share of the Gross National Product (GNP) increased by more than 52 percent between 1960 and 1975—a period when the GNP originated by government increased by 26 percent and the share originated by business declined by almost 6 percent.

The steady growth of the nonprofit sector is accompanied by new and increasingly more complex methods of raising money and managing nonprofit organizations. This book is designed to assist practitioners serving young children and their families in becoming familiar with some of these methods and competent in obtaining financial support.

Many programs for young children—home visitation projects for families with children under three, information and referral networks, services for handicapped infants and preschoolers, parent support groups, day care centers, etc.—were developed through federal initiatives and often with federal funds. The reliance on public support has left many such programs not only dependent on government grants, but also ignorant of new developments in the field of fundraising and of the options available for the support of services.

Given continuing indications of dwindling public funds—prolonged periods of inflation and depression, a sluggish economy, massive budget cuts, and changes in public funding practices—the future of many child and family services appears to be gloomy. Several such services have been eliminated by the severe budget cuts; many others are threatened with extinction. In order to survive during the coming decade, those of us who direct and coordinate programs for young children must change the ways we have been operating.

First, we must forge new and in some ways different relations with the public sector. New, because it is no longer the federal government that we must look to for child and family policy issues, but the state governments, since it is they who now bear the responsibility for deciding on priorities and allocating funds. Different, because we must finally accept the fact that public funds are limited and seek other avenues for the support of programs.

Second, we must acquire fundraising skills and use creativity and ingenuity in implementing these skills. During these economically lean years, it is not only government funds which are limited but also the money allocated for philanthropy by the private sector. What is more, the number of causes needing support and the number of applicants for funds are soaring. Those looking for money in support of programs and services must be prepared to meet powerful competition. They should be competent in their own fields, and they must also be skilled in identifying likely sources of funds and able to make written and oral presentations that stand out.

There are many books on getting grants, on winning corporate support, and on tested ways of successful fundraising. Some are written for the novice, some for the expert. Although this book will serve as an introduction to some of these books, it is different in that it is written with programs for young children specifically in mind. Also, the emphasis here is not on telling how to get a foundation grant or a corporate contribution, although these topics are included, but on instilling the idea that fundraising is an essential, perennial component of child care services.

What you will find in this book are techniques also used by large nonprofit organizations such as universities, institutions, and hospitals, all of which have a built-in fundraising component. The methods used by these organizations are by no means new. They have been reworked and refined over the years and used in a variety of ways. What is new is their applicability in helping relatively small programs and services for children and families become self-sustaining and independent.

Acknowledgments

I would like to extend my sincere thanks to my husband, J. John Stevenson, Esq., and to Henry C. Suhrke, both from *Philanthropy Monthly*, for their counsel and support throughout the writing of this book. I also appreciate the dedication and help of Carol Buell, from the Bush Center in Child Development and Social Policy at Yale, in the preparation of the manuscript. Finally, I would like to acknowledge the Bush Foundation, St. Paul, Minnesota, which facilitates my work at the Yale Bush Center.

M. F.

Fundraising: An introduction

Fundraising is the art of obtaining money or other assets from government, individuals, organizations, foundations, and business firms for the benefit of nonprofit organizations.

Although charity and therefore the practice of raising money or other means of helping others are traditional, fundraising has become an increasingly organized and specialized field. Several changes account for this development.

First, during the 1930s, some large nonprofit organizations discovered that it was worthwhile to employ an individual to concentrate on soliciting contributions from individual donors. Before that time, fundraising was largely the effort of volunteers. While the role of volunteers in fundraising and in other phases of managing a nonprofit organization remains strong even today, most large such organizations employ not one, but several people whose task it is to raise funds or oversee and coordinate in-house fundraising efforts. There are also a number of professional firms available to provide advice or services as well as professional organizations of fundraisers, such as the National Society of Fund Raising Executives.

Second, fundraising today has become not only a profession but also a professional endeavor, and for good reason. With increased taxation since World War II, which meant that private incomes no longer had as much cash to spare for philanthropy, there was increased competition for contributions. Charities began looking for funds not only among individuals but also among businesses and corporations. Fundraising efforts became more intense and also more creative. Principles from advertising and marketing are incorporated into the appeal for funds; motivations for giving are researched; and systems for solicitations are developed and refined.

Accompanying these changes has been the development of myriad laws and regulations governing charitable solicitations. These differ from state to state and are enforced primarily to reassure the public that their contributions are not spent on the process of fundraising, but mostly on the cause the organization promotes. Fundraisers, as professionals, are also held accountable by their peers and are developing an accreditation system.

Definitions of terms

To provide an introduction to developments and options in fundraising, let us define some of the terms used. These will give you an idea of the range of possibilities in the field and will present some of the principles and elements of the art of raising money as they will be discussed in the book:

annual appeal—a campaign, conducted once each year, to raise operating funds for a nonprofit organization.

annuity—amount of money derived from insurance or a trust fund payable annually or at other regular intervals.

bequest—that which is left by a will, usually a set amount of money or a percentage of an estate.

bequeath—to leave money or personal property by will.

campaign—also known as a *fund drive*, an organized method for obtaining money. There are many types of campaigns. A *capital campaign*, for example, is conducted occasionally in order to obtain money for buildings, land, equipment, or endowment. It differs from the *annual appeal*, which is conducted to raise money for current operations.

charitable lead trust—a trust established whereby income is paid to a charity for a designated number of years at the termination of which the trust principal is paid over to the heirs of the donors.

charitable remainder annuity trust—a trust established whereby *the donor* receives a fixed amount of money annually for life or for not more than 20 years; upon the death of the donor, the principal reverts to a charity named.

charitable remainder unitrust — a trust established whereby a donor receives a fixed percentage of the fair market value of the trust's assets for life or for not more than 20 years; upon the death of the donor, the principal reverts to the charity named by the donor.

contribution—a gift to a religious or nonprofit organization for which no tangible value is received. A contribution may be in money, property, or in other form.

deferred giving—contributing to an organization other than by current gifts; funds are designated to be given to the organization at a later date.

devise—to distribute or to give real estate by will.

direct mail solicitation—asking individuals for contributions through the mail.

donor—a person who contributes to a religious or nonprofit organization. Also referred to as *contributor*, or *giver*.

endowment—a process whereby a donor provides funds to an organization, the investment income of which can be used to operate a facility or a program. This term also refers to a payment to the insured of the fair amount of an insurance policy after a stated period of time.

estate planning—a systematic review of legal and tax aspects of the disposition of real and personal property, assets, insurance, securities, pensions, legacies, and trusts to insure that an individual's own priority concerns for her or his family and charitable interests are put into effect at the time of her or his death.

federated campaign—a campaign conducted by one agency or group for several participating member organizations. The United Way is a federated campaign.

fundraiser—a person who obtains money for a nonprofit organization. In most cases, the term applies to people who are hired to help others (volunteers or staff) raise money. Some organizations have a fundraiser on their staff, usually referred to as a program development director/officer. The term is sometimes used to denote a fundraising event.

grant—allocation of money by a foundation, corporation, government, or other organization to an individual or nonprofit organization for a specifically stated purpose.

in-plant solicitation—a fundraising campaign within one or more businesses for a particular organization, or for several organizations.

inter vivos trust — a living trust created by a donor for specific purposes for a period of time. A charity may be named as beneficiary for a period of ten years or more. This is a tax saving opportunity for the creator of the trust.

legacy—same as *bequest*.

life insurance policy—a contract in which an insurance company agrees to pay an agreed upon sum of money to a beneficiary, which may be a nonprofit organization, upon death of the insured.

matching funds—(1) a government, foundation, or corporate grant awarded contingent upon the agency's raising a specific or equal amount of money and (2) that specific or equal amount of money. The term may also be used in conjunction with a campaign in cases where donors make contributions that are contingent upon the nonprofit organization's ability to raise a certain amount of money from other sources.

memorial—anything intended to preserve the memory of a person or event. Memorial gifts, in money or otherwise, are made to nonprofit organizations to memorialize a deceased person.

pledge—a promise made by a potential donor to pay a specific sum over a set period of time or at a later date.

pooled income—property transferred to charity is comingled with property contributed or assigned by other donors and from which each donor receives a lifetime interest.

residual bequest—after a donor assigns legacies to heirs and friends, all or part of that which remains becomes the residual, or remainder, of the bequest, which may be given to the charity of the donor's choice.

restricted bequest—gifts to a charity through a will which specifies the purpose of the gift or how it must be used. For example, a donor may leave an amount of money to a hospital to be used *only* as an endowment, the income from the principal of which is to be used for projects or programs relating to newborn infants.

solicitor—a volunteer, paid staff person, or hired consultant who is involved in fundraising or asking for contributions.

testamentary trust—a trust established by a last will and testament.

trust fund—real or personal property, money, or assets held and managed by one person or one institution for the benefit of another.

Implications for your organization

Several principles emerge from a review of the terms defined.

1. Fundraising is much more complicated than applying for and receiving a foundation, corporate, or government grant.
2. The individual donor is the emphasis of many fundraising efforts.
3. Creative arrangements may be made between the donor and the charitable organization to the benefit of both parties.
4. A contribution does not have to be in cash to be meaningful.
5. A contribution does not have to be immediate. Soliciting gifts to be contributed at a later date, as in deferred giving, provides nonprofit organizations the opportunity for long-range planning.

W here does your organization start?

Whether your organization is well established or newly created, you can develop a viable fundraising program. One of the first and most important steps you have to take toward this end is to look at fundraising not as a one-time, limited activity—such as responding to a government-sponsored request for proposal (RFP)—but as a constant and important aspect of organization management.

Programs for young children in particular may need to adjust their concepts of administration. Many such programs have been dependent on government support since their inception and thus may be in an immediate predicament. It is not an unusual occurrence, for example, for organizations to find out, upon a week's or month's notice, that the grant submitted to a government agency is not to be funded. This leaves the organization without operating funds and with insufficient time to look for other avenues of support. There is often no other course but for the staff to find other jobs and for the organization to fold. Unfortunately, too many fine programs have met their end just this way.

Dependence on the public sector also means that programs remain limited in scope. A government grant often covers only the basics— salaries, rent, utilities, or even less; there are many projects which operate with donated space because rent is not covered in their grants. With limited budgets, the potential for growth in size or quality of many child and family programs is never realized.

Operating on a skeletal budget can change once you build a permanent fundraising component into your program. But how do you begin?

Basic knowledge of fundraising methods and techniques is an important prerequisite to successful implementation of a fundraising component. But it is not enough. Other requirements include money and time. How much of either is necessary will depend on the type of organization you have, the composition and responsibilities of your staff, the availability of volunteers, the availability and responsibility of your board of directors, and so on. The money you raise will increase in relation to your organizational structure, the amount of money and effort invested, and your decision to employ one inexperienced person on a trial-and-error basis or experts in the field.

But it can be done. Before I go on, I will help you analyze your particular situation through a series of questions you must ask yourself.

Has your organization received a nonprofit corporation charter from the state? Have you applied for IRS tax exemption?

It is important that the answer to both questions be yes. Established programs, especially those which receive public support, are probably nonprofit corporations. Those that are not formally chartered should contact the Office of the Secretary of State or other appropriate state department to determine how to incorporate.

If your organization does not have an IRS tax exemption, you should fill out IRS Form 1023, followed in some cases by IRS Form 990. Guidelines on application procedures are available in IRS Publication 557 and Package 1023. These are available at your local IRS office.

Acquiring nonprofit status and tax exemption is important. Without nonprofit status you will not be eligible to receive foundation money, for example, and depending on laws governing donations in your state you may be prohibited from certain fundraising activities. Without an IRS exemption letter, donors will not be able to declare their gifts as deductible from their income and thus will be less likely to contribute to your organization.

Many organizations which serve children may encounter difficulties with the IRS in obtaining recognition of their tax-exempt status. This is partly because the IRS may not be aware of the implications of new ideas in child development and education. Day care centers (Bromberg 1979) and early childhood programs may find it particularly difficult to get a tax exemption because the IRS views services of these programs as primarily custodial. Quality early childhood programs do provide education; they have a curriculum to further children's cognitive development; they offer activities to enhance the children's development of social competence. Thus they are educational rather than custodial in nature, and should be entitled to receive the IRS exemption. Programs have successfully appealed an IRS ruling (see, for example, San Francisco Infant School v. Commissioner, 69 T.C. No. 83, March 20, 1978).

Do you have a board of directors?

According to a recent study (Greater New York Fund/United Way 1980), the number of directors on the boards of nonprofit organizations can be in the hundreds while in regular, for-profit corporations, for example Ford Motor Company, the average number of directors is in the twenties. The implication is that the functions of the two types of boards are very different. Unlike the for-profit corporation's board, the trustees or directors of nonprofit organizations are needed not only for or primarily for management or policy-setting purposes, but also to help increase the organization's potential to raise funds. The more directors, then, the larger the potential (but don't go overboard).

In the case of an organization such as a day care center, size and effectiveness of the board may be increased by inviting the participation of other individuals. As you build a board, it is important to work with current members as much as possible, and to draw on their knowledge and contacts. Some of them may be parents who work in a large corporation whose president or chair they may be able to approach as a possible new member of the board or donor. Others may know a prominent member of the community or they may have helped promote the candidacy of a political figure whom you may consider to be a valuable asset to your organization.

Some programs for children and families may be operated within the context of a larger organization—a school or hospital. If this is the case with your program, you may want to look at the structure of that organization's board and its members and draw upon them for support, if at all possible. In cases where the larger organization is the local educational agency, members of the school board may not be supportive of all programs, for example, birth-to-three child care. Some may not even consider such a program an appropriate educational endeavor. If you have neither your own board of directors, nor the support of the sponsoring organization's board, consider forming an advisory committee for your particular program. This committee may be made up of a number of supportive individuals who can help you in fundraising, policy-setting, and public relations activities.

As you develop a list of prospective board or advisory committee members, it may be helpful to you and your current board members and staff to consider individuals in terms of what they can contribute to the organization, and their interest in your cause. Lawyers and accountants are often members of the boards of nonprofit organizations because of their interest as well as their expertise and skills; some organizations may include other experts. For example, an organization serving learning disabled children may have a pediatrician or an ophthalmologist on the board. Some organizations invite wealthy or prestigious individuals to join their board because of their local or national recognition and ability to draw on others to follow their example and support the organization.

Prospective board members should also be considered for their interest in the program's cause so they can contribute enthusiasm, initiative, and willingness to help. In order to find out if the individuals will be interested, you will have to know a little about their background. Any incidental point may be of help to you. For example, the wife of the chairman of a major firm based in Dayton, Ohio, was working on a master's degree in early childhood education at a time when some individuals considered opening a day care center. They approached her with the idea. Not very much later, the chairman and his staff were working on opening a corporate-based day care center. There are other examples: a prominent legislator who is the parent of a Down syndrome child enthusiastically supports a home visitation program for young handicapped children; a family with three children who have had difficulties with school supports programs and services for learning disabled children.

What is your case?

As you get more deeply involved in fundraising, you will realize that most people are generous when asked to support a cause, a project, a program, or a service but not necessarily an organization.

What you do as an organization—home visits, parent education, child care—is your program. Why you are doing it, when, where, for whom, with whom, with what funds, goals and objectives, effectiveness—all these and more contribute to a good program. The case for support is drawn from the program.

People will ask: Why should we support your program and how much should we contribute? Depending on the particular solicitation approach you use and the constituency you solicit, you will have different ways of answering these questions. The literature you prepare to aid you in solicitation efforts will also highlight different aspects of your program and your appeal. However, one concise statement—called the case statement—should pull all these aspects together.

Before you venture into the community, look over the reasons, or needs, upon which you base your program. Review the goals and objectives of your organization. Do these adequately describe your program? If not, work on them to develop a clear statement of cause, purpose, and functions. This is your case statement.

What is your budget?

As mentioned earlier, you need money to raise money. The amount of money you can expect to raise depends on the amount of money and effort you spend. It also determines which fundraising activities you will initiate first. If you have $2,000 in your budget to spend on fundraising, obviously you cannot begin a direct mail solicitation or a large capital campaign. But you may be able to use that amount of money to sponsor a series of smaller events such as teas, raffles, etc., which can generate more money that can be used to sponsor other fundraising efforts.

Related to the budget question are the matters of time and human resources. Is yours a three-member, parent training program with one of the staff serving as teacher/director? If so, how much staff time do you honestly believe you can allow for seeking support? Are there any volunteers you can appeal to to teach in order to free staff time for raising money, or volunteers you can ask to actually solicit money for the program? Your first activity may well be to enlist volunteers.

Is yours an organization with several staff members, a director, and a board of directors? If so, the director's time may be sufficiently flexible to include coordination of fundraising activities and several members of the board of directors may also be available to help. Even so, some priorities will have to be set. Which of the director's activities can be eliminated or delegated in order to allow for more time to seek support?

Visiting the homes of newly registered children might wait, or responsibilities for staff development sessions could be delegated to one or
several of the teachers on a rotating basis.

You may determine that you have neither money nor time to activate
a viable fundraising program within your organization. What then?
Should you give up the idea and continue to operate on a meager and
insecure funding base? Not at all. It is possible to begin on a small scale,
and it has been done. What you need is patience, persistence, and
ingenuity.

One successful way to start is to seek seed money in order to build a
fundraising program. Seed money may be available from your community foundation or a corporation (see Chapter 4) and finding it may entail
a small percentage of your time and effort. It is worthwhile for it not
only provides money, or frees your time so that you can acquire fundraising skills or seek expert help, but it also gives you the opportunity,
as you write the proposal for funding, to spell out your project's agenda
for action.

Networking is another option. If yours is one of several similar
programs in the community, why not form a network? Meet with the
directors of other programs and find out if they are willing to join forces
to raise money together. As a collective unit you will be representative
of larger numbers and more likely to gain the attention of prospective
donors. You will find, too, that there is more time among several of you
so you can divide tasks accordingly. You may also be able to convince a
group of volunteers, such as retired people, a civic group, etc., to help.

Why are you raising money?

After you have analyzed your particular organizational structure by
answering the preceding questions and are ready to venture into the
task of fundraising, this question remains: What—specifically—are you
raising money for?

Nonprofit organizations look for money to finance a program or service; to build or to rent facilities; or to develop and to implement
activities. Or, they may have part of the money required for a particular
project and may be looking for matching funds. Some donors, for exam-

ple, make substantial contributions to an organization in order to stimulate others to give; by stipulating that the money will be donated only if a certain amount of money is raised from other sources, they encourage the organization to look elsewhere for support and to be an incentive for other donors to contribute.

Whatever reason you have for fundraising must be clearly identified not only for your own benefit, for this is likely to help you in choosing the appropriate fundraising method, but for the benefit of prospective donors as well. People want to know specifically how their money is used. Just as you have to make a clear statement of purpose describing the goals of your organization—your case statement—so you have to indicate how you plan to spend the money raised.

Once you begin fundraising and become self-sufficient as an organization, you will conduct activities on a regular basis: an annual drive, an occasional capital campaign, etc. You will find that your reasons for raising funds change over the years. Some important reasons for fundraising may not be directly related to money. Some organizations, for example, regard a campaign not only as a good way to raise money, but also as an effective way of increasing the visibility of an organization in the community. A campaign may also help the organization develop prestige and status in the community, especially if the organizers are able to attract socially prominent people to help them solicit the support and contributions of others. Other organizations recognize a fundraising campaign as an effective way to educate the public about a problem or inform the public about conditions.

In any fundraising effort, you must have a case to sell. Your case statement will tell, for example, of the increasing numbers of abused children in the nation as a whole and in the community, or of your capability to prevent many handicapping conditions through programs for pregnant women. With programs for young children, informing the public about the needs of children will serve as a powerful instrument in helping promote the children's cause.

Implications for your organization

Fundraising, as you can see, must be an integral and active part of your organization just as are other components which make up your program. Beyond providing you with a firm basis of support, it is also an effective way for you to:

- structure your program
- define your purpose
- sell your case
- promote your cause

3
What are some ways to raise money?

Most Americans believe it is their duty to support nonprofit educational and/or humanitarian organizations. Also, to be able to contribute to and to be associated prominently with leading organizations of this kind confers a high degree of social status. It is against this background that the field of philanthropy in America has grown and fundraising has evolved as a profession.

Methods for getting people to support philanthropic causes vary from organization to organization. Nonprofit organizations may use not one but several methods of raising funds. Universities and colleges, for example, depend on the support of their alumni, but they also look for corporate and foundation support for faculty development and research. Many other organizations depend on an annual fund drive—a regular event or set of activities which produces funds, although when it is required they may also launch a campaign to raise capital for a building or to generate endowment. The campaign may include personal solicitations, use of the mass media to advertise need for donations, direct mail solicitation, and contributions from foundations and corporations.

As you begin to develop a fundraising component for your program, you will learn a great deal about what options you have for raising funds by finding out what other organizations do to raise money. A word of caution, however: What works successfully for one organization may not work for yours. Therefore, you should not only find out what other organizations are doing, you should also analyze each fundraising method and technique in terms of your own particular situation. Ask yourself these questions:

1. How much money do I have to spend on generating funds?
2. What would the activity demand in terms of money, time, materials, and preparation?

3. Is the activity too expensive to be implemented successfully?
4. Is the activity appropriate for the community?
5. What is the program's visibility in the community? Do enough people know about it to come out in support of its cause?
6. How much time will be involved and do I have the time?
7. Do I have the staff necessary to carry out the activity?
8. Would the activity be more successful if I sought professional fundraising counsel?
9. Do I have enough money to hire fundraising professionals?

The answers to these questions will help you decide which activity is appropriate for your particular program. As you learn more about your organization's potential to attract support, you will be able to implement a series of successful activities, possibly selected from those discussed in the remainder of this chapter that are especially applicable to organizations serving children and families.

Grants

A grant entails the allocation of money, usually by a foundation, corporation, or government agency, to a nonprofit organization for a specifically stated purpose. Most nonprofit organizations include grants among their methods of soliciting support. Hospitals, colleges, and schools depend on government and foundation grants for research and other specific projects, although they also conduct a variety of other fundraising events.

Special events

Schools, churches, and charitable organizations depend on one regular event a year not only to raise funds but also for public relations and visibility in the community, or they sometimes schedule several such events during the course of the year, if that can be done. Churches, for example, have the space and volunteers to conduct large dinners or breakfasts as fundraisers three or four times a year. These not only help support the church but are also important as community social events.

Here is a list of some activities you may consider. It is by no means an exhaustive list, of course, but it will give you and your staff a start upon which to build:

golf tournament	bingo party
coffee morning	antique sale and auction
fashion show	holiday craft or food fair
bridge drive	concert
car rally	wine-tasting party
flower show	pancake breakfast
tag (garage) sale	dinner dance
wine and cheese gathering	Las Vegas night
raffle	competition

This type of event can generate anywhere from $100 to $10,000. It can also become much more complex. A bingo party, for example, may become a weekly endeavor. Churches look to bingo games as a regular source of income. But you must proceed with caution and you should seek legal counsel if you are thinking of promoting such an event on a frequent and regular basis. State laws and regulations differ: some allow only religious organizations to hold bingo games; others allow any nonprofit organization to do so as long as (1) it has been in existence in the state for a specified length of time and (2) it has received a license from the state granting permission to conduct such activities.

Another relatively simple fundraising event that is becoming more complex in a legal sense is the raffle. Enterprising homeowners and nonprofit organizations have taken advantage of the slow housing market to suit both parties. A couple from Fairfax, Virginia, unable to sell their home, contacted a nonprofit organization which in turn agreed to raffle their home. Tickets sold at $100, which was considered a donation to the nonprofit organization. From the proceeds, the organization paid the homeowners the price they were asking for the house and kept the rest. One lucky member of the community won a house and the organization raised a notable sum.

Soon after this happened, many organizations sponsored house raffles. Some even advertised for homeowners who wanted to sell their houses that way. Several churches and other organizations actually raffled houses, with the proceeds to the organization often reaching $100,000. Again, you have to act with caution. The local police or the state may regard this sort of event as an illegal form of gambling. In Ohio, there was a ruling prohibiting the raffle of houses by nonprofit organizations. In Connecticut, however, it is legal to do so if the proceeds go toward halfway or shelter homes, although there is extensive lobbying to change the laws to allow all nonprofit and religious organizations to be able to promote a house raffle.

We highlight these activities for two reasons: (1) to illustrate the legal issues surrounding fundraising and impress upon the reader the necessity of checking the legal implications of activities before proceeding further and (2) to illustrate the creativity involved in fundraising and how, through need and ingenuity, fundraising events can take on new significance.

How to select a special event

Special events can generate a significant amount of money and also help promote the visibility of your organization. Staging one such event may well get you off to a good start toward creating a fundraising component in your organization. Choose the event carefully, however, so that it is:

1. in keeping with what the community will support; you know your area best and the general makeup of the population. If there are many retired residents of the community, a morning coffee would be suitable; if there are more young families, a pancake breakfast would generate more attendance.
2. of interest to your staff members and volunteers. This is especially important for the small program which will be dependent, for a while at least, on the help of its staff and volunteers.

Who will hold the special event?

Many organizations depend on their own staff members or volunteers to help stage a special event. In these cases, you may find it important to appoint a committee that would be responsible for the event. You may be able to recruit volunteers to help you and your staff promote an event which, of course, would be ideal. Alternatively, you may choose a professional organization or person to conduct the event on behalf of your organization. Choose the person(s) carefully, however; ask for references and inquire about expertise, background, and credibility.

Annual giving

Annual giving refers to the method of raising operating funds for an organization every year, often through a variety of approaches such as direct mail and personal solicitations. The annual appeal is dependent in large part on past donors (with emphasis on acquiring larger gifts from them each year) and acquiring new contributors.

Although the term annual giving denotes a once-a-year event, it should be regarded as continuous, especially in the case of newly formed organizations or those organizations which are just beginning to institute a fundraising component. This is not to say that donors should be continuously asked to contribute. On the contrary, your appeal should be made on an annual basis only, or else you risk losing the donor. Some veteran fundraisers may disagree with this notion and contend that to ask a donor to contribute to an annual appeal jeopardizes the opportunity to receive other gifts from the same donor during the year. In order not to jeopardize these opportunities and also not to risk losing the donor's support altogether, some organizations do not refer to the appeal as annual, but approach the donor only once a year. The preparation for the annual appeal and the acquisition of new donors should be a constant process at least until you have a good list of supporters.

Capital campaigns

The capital campaign is a method of periodically raising money for a specific project or purpose: to build a new wing, to acquire a building or large equipment, for endowment, etc. The capital campaign has a higher funding goal than does the annual appeal, and is therefore dependent on larger individual gifts.

Organizations would not normally become involved in capital campaigns until they have built up an adequate base of supporters and are reasonably sure of the success of the campaign. Often, it is advisable to conduct a feasibility study to determine the organization's potential to raise money in the community before launching a capital campaign, simply because of the requirements of time and money associated with the effort.

Federated campaigns

Some organizations opt to raise money collectively, i.e., through another umbrella group which exists specifically to raise money for its member organizations. The most notable example of this is the United Way of America. Other examples are the Federation of Protestant Welfare Agencies, Catholic Charities, and United Jewish Appeal. Some of these are national in scope; others cover only local organizations.

There are advantages and disadvantages to joining a federated campaign. On the positive side, (1) joining absolves an organization from much of the work involved in raising money; (2) it may be highly effective for an organization that is small or relatively unknown and thus less likely to be successful in raising money on its own; and (3) one appeal on behalf of several groups may be better received than approaching donors a number of times.

On the negative side, the disadvantages are: (1) there is often competition for funds even within federated groups, with the smaller organizations frequently feeling that they are inadequately supported; (2) growth and independence of the smaller organizations may be inhibited because in a federated campaign the money is usually allocated to member organizations on the basis of their size, so a smaller organization is likely to receive smaller amounts; and (3) the opportunities to involve the community in the support of the organization and to increase the organization's visibility are minimized.

In order to determine if your organization should seek federated financing, you should obtain clear answers to these questions:

1. How much money is your organization likely to get?

2. Would your organization remain free of controls imposed by the umbrella group?

3. Would your organization be able to conduct additional public relations and fundraising efforts on its own?

Deferred giving

Deferred giving, sometimes also referred to as planned giving, is becoming more and more prevalent as a way of raising money to support nonprofit organizations. Briefly defined, deferred giving is a way to contribute to an organization by having funds come to an organization after a donor has received her or his tax deductibility. This method of soliciting support is attractive both to the organization and to the donor because it promotes the notion of future financial security for the organization, and encourages donors who may not be in the position to make current contributions.

There are various ways donors may participate in a deferred giving program of an organization, including (1) lifetime-income plans that allow the donor to receive lifetime income from securities which are turned over to the charity upon the donor's death; (2) transferring ownership of real estate to a charitable organization while maintaining lifetime use of the property; (3) instituting a charitable lead trust which pays a designated income to the nonprofit organization for a designated number of years at the termination of which the trust principal is paid over to the heirs of the donors; and (4) naming a charitable organization as a beneficiary in a will.

These are just some ways deferred-giving gifts may be made. As you can see, they can be quite complicated and are usually handled either by law firms or banks, many of which have departments specializing in providing just such assistance to nonprofit organizations.

Memorial giving

Memorial gifts are made to nonprofit organizations in remembrance of a deceased person. Many people find it a meaningful way to express condolences. In order to be successful, however, preparation must be made, including, of course, informing the public of an organization's memorial gift program, printing of memorial envelopes and donor receipts, etc. Once established, it can be an effective way of maintaining support for an organization.

Mail appeals

One way of soliciting contributions from individual donors is through personal contact. Another way is by letter. Obviously direct mail solicitation reaches many more individuals in a given time period. The likelihood of getting a contribution via direct mail is not as good as via personal contact. Many organizations, therefore, use mail appeals as one of several methods of fundraising, usually in concert with publicity and other activities that make up a campaign.

There are two important factors in a mail appeal, the letter and the selection of individuals to whom the letter will be sent. The letter should include the same basic information provided for a potential donor in person: what the cause is, what the agency has accomplished, why you are writing, how the money the donor contributes will be used, etc. In addition to the letter, you may want to send brochures or other informative literature to further enhance your appeal and to satisfy the reader's curiosity about the organization.

The individuals who receive the letter should be those likely to sympathize with the cause in question. These may include members of your organization, parents and relatives of the children you serve, correspondents of your organization, and well-known business and philanthropic leaders.

Lists of individuals are available for rental if you are contemplating a mass mailing on a national basis. Such lists may be categorized by age or occupation, for example, and are purchased from list brokers or associations. In order to use a mailing list, however, you must first determine which individuals are most likely to contribute.

The expense associated with extensive direct mail solicitations—the postage, printing, rental of lists, nurturing of donors, etc.—has resulted in techniques which serve to increase efficiency, control, and the likelihood of successfully selecting donors. Before considering this method, care should be taken to discuss with an expert cost, these various techniques, your organization's potential to raise funds in this way, and the legal implications involved.

Sources of support 4

Knowing about the various fundraising methods, some of which are discussed in the previous chapter, is important. Equally important is knowing what are the sources of support and techniques to be used in soliciting funds.

Money or other forms of support are given to philanthropic organizations by individual donors, corporations, foundations, and government agencies. Ideally, a nonprofit organization would rely on all four sources, thereby insuring financial stability and growth. Some organizations do not. Many programs for young children and their families have depended nearly totally on government support. The role of foundations and corporations in the support of social services is becoming increasingly significant as government funding becomes less available. The support of individual donors, however, is rarely acknowledged, despite the fact that more than 75 percent of all charitable contributions is made by individuals (American Association of Fund Raising Counsel, Inc. 1981).

The discussion that follows will emphasize the role of each of these sources in the support of organizations serving young children, what you need to know about approaching each of these sources, and how you can most effectively use them to benefit your organization.

Individual donors

Individual donors are the backbone of a variety of fundraising methods ranging from the simple special event, which they may support as part of their community obligation or social life, to the more complex campaigns, deferred giving, and direct mail solicitations. Individual donors, those who donate small amounts as well as those who make significant contributions, are sought, studied, and approached by hospitals, colleges, and large charities. These institutions methodically keep lists of individuals, their backgrounds, and the amount they contribute; they use this information over and over again as part of annual appeals and capital campaigns.

Thus far social service organizations, perhaps because of their reliance on grants, fail to recognize the individual donor's potential for support. There are many ways individuals may contribute their support:

- as volunteers
- as members of the board of directors
- as contributors of current gifts
- as participants of a deferred giving program

As you develop a viable fundraising program in your organization, you may involve individuals in all these ways. Until then you will want to focus your efforts (1) on convincing key individuals of the importance of your cause and (2) on seeking their support not only financially, but also as volunteers or members of the board of directors.

Identify prospects

The individuals you approach first should be interested in the cause and capable of influencing others to support your organization. Who are your likely prospects? They may be wealthy or prestigious individuals in the community, chief executive officers of nearby corporations, political figures, prominent social club members, business people in the community, etc. The emphasis here on attracting influential people needs some explanation. I am not suggesting that in philanthropy only individuals of means and influence can help you but I do suggest that you attract a few such individuals in order to increase the visibility and credibility of your particular organization and to acquire a base of support with more speed.

In addition, the contributions of other individual donors should not be minimized. Gifts of $25 and less account for a large portion of all money donated by individuals. It will be advantageous to seek all types of

donors and to respond to those who contribute smal'
courtesy and respect in anticipation of their potential to conti....
in the future.

Solicit contributions

Once you have a list of prospective donors who are likely to make
significant donations and/or lend their support in other ways you will be
ready to approach them. Remember that you are approaching these
individuals for a contribution of both money and time.

As you begin the solicitation, you should abide by the following
guidelines:

1. See prospective donors in person at a time and place convenient to
   them. Professional conduct is essential.
2. Be proud of your organization and do not feel you are begging.
   Novice solicitors may take a while to feel proud of their task,
   although they eventually do. Remember that you are not requesting money for yourself, but for your organization, and a cause
   which you firmly believe in.
3. Present your case concisely but thoroughly: why are you there,
   what is the purpose of your appeal, what is your cause or program.
   Stress the latter, as you will find it easier to ask people for money
   for causes or projects than for an organization (see Chapter 2).
4. Do not underestimate the prospective donor's generosity and ability to pay. Most people feel flattered about being asked to contribute a large amount of money. If they cannot do so, they will simply
   tell you that they can contribute a different amount.
5. Make your visit short and try not to get involved in prolonged
   discussions about anything not related to the main purpose of your
   visit.
6. Leave informative literature about your organization with each
   prospective donor.
7. Thank, by letter, each of the prospective donors you met with even
   if some did not give any money or acknowledge their willingness to
   otherwise support your cause. Remember that they may be in a
   better position to support you the following year.
8. Keep accurate records of all your personal solicitation activities.
   An organized way to do this is to maintain a card file on each of the

prospective donors, specifying how much if any was contributed, etc. Basic information such as this will be valuable for contacts in following years and will be the basis of annual appeals should you decide to have these.

Corporations

With diminishing government support of social services came the hope that the private sector, corporations and private foundations, would provide needed human services. Both corporations and foundations may seem to be attractive sources of support to the novice. The potential may be there—not necessarily for long-term support, but perhaps for programs to begin to be independent and to institute their permanent fundraising component. Remember, however, that the competition for funds is likely to be tough. Other organizations, from small early childhood programs to large universities and hospitals, were badly hurt by the government budget cuts and are working to forge new ties, or strengthen old ones, with the private sector.

As a nonprofit institution, you should be aware of two points with regard to corporate giving:

1. Corporations as a rule do not like to make charitable contributions.
2. The tax saving as a motivation for giving is meaningless to corporations.

These two points may be surprising to many, but only 6 percent of all corporations make contributions amounting to $500 or more a year (The Conference Board 1981). Furthermore, corporate contributions, which amount to $1 billion a year, represent less than 1 percent of corporate annual gross profits (American Association of Fund Raising Counsel, Inc. 1981) although for many years the IRS allowed corporations to use as much as 5 percent of the annual gross profits in deductions for charitable contributions, and in 1982 allowed 10 percent.

Corporate philanthropy is an elusive field. It is extremely difficult to elicit information on the amount or nature of corporate donations. Those in corporations who are in charge of administering donations, individuals often referred to as corporate contributions officers, represent a tiny function of the company. The principal company purpose—sometimes engaging thousands of individuals—is to produce income for the company and its stockholders. Thus, not only do they represent a minority corporate interest but they often do not have the time or the staff to find out if an organization approaching them for funding is credible, nor do they have the knowledge to judge whether the program or project they are asked to support is worthwhile or necessary. Understanding and appreciating these constraints will help the grant-seeker in deciding on an appropriate approach.

Despite these facts, soliciting corporations may be an easier task than soliciting a foundation. First, corporations are more accessible in that they are in, or in close proximity to, many communities whereas foundations are concentrated in New York City and other metropolitan areas (except, of course, community foundations). Second, most corporations are informal in their approach to contributing, and many do not have specific requirements such as deadlines for proposals or funding policies. However, extensive research is as important in this case as it is with fundraising from other sources.

Soliciting corporate support

There are three important phases in the process of soliciting corporate support:

Identify the corporations to approach. This should not be too difficult, because the closer the applicant organization is to the corporation, the more likely it is to be funded. A first step would be to list all the corporations in the area.

Find out who to approach within the corporation. An important rule in corporate and foundation fundraising is to locate an internal champion. Try to pinpoint someone, preferably on the board of directors, who knows of the applicant organization or who is sensitive to the purposes of the program, or cause, to be funded.

Sources of information about corporations and their personnel include corporate directories published by local chambers of commerce. For in-depth profiles on corporate activities and interests of top-level management, there are corporate annual reports (available in business schools or universities, or sometimes through brokerage firms). Local libraries, even in small communities, often keep extensive profiles on prestigious community members; some may be serving on the boards of corporations. Other sources of information are *Standard and Poor's Register of Corporations, Directors and Executives, Who's Who in America* and *Who's Who in Finance and Industry*. These provide information about home town, school, awards, offices, boards, and other community affiliations of company management.

Securing this type of information may seem trivial and irrelevant. It is neither. The more one knows about top management level personnel, and about the corporation's activities, the more likely one will be to identify an internal champion and to appeal to the needs and interests of the corporation, thus increasing the chances of getting support.

Suppose that you have researched a corporation and the list of executives does not generate someone who knows of the applicant organization or its staff. What then? The next step is to contact someone in the organization who is in charge of corporate contributions. This person's name is usually not widely advertised. A common mistake made by grant-seekers is to assume that the corporate contributions officer is part of the public relations department. This is the case only in some companies. If a grant-seeker's initial request to speak with someone connected with philanthropy results in an inappropriate response, it is advisable to contact the president's office. The president of a corporation may not be the right person to contact, but she or he or the secretary can refer you to the appropriate individual.

Determine what kind of support you are looking for. Remember that corporate support does not have to be money in order to be useful to your organization. One school in Ohio, for example, was looking for a modest sum of money for playground equipment for an early childhood program for the handicapped. They contacted the person in charge of corporate contributions for a large fast-food chain in the midwest. That person was not very enthusiastic about donating $2,000 for a program which was relatively unknown and which served only a handful of children. However, he happened to be in charge of the company's public awareness program and recognized the opportunity for media coverage and a philanthropic endeavor. What he arranged for the school far exceeded its expectations. He launched a citywide, much-publicized campaign whereby half of the proceeds from the sale of hamburgers for a period of time were donated to the school for the purpose of providing a playground for handicapped preschoolers. In addition, the services of a team of architects of the food chain were donated. The architects designed a playground for the specific needs of the children, and also for the school—the playground was mobile so that in case the school building was closed down, the playground could be easily relocated.

There are numerous ways a corporation may be helpful to programs for young children and their families that do not involve an actual transfer of dollars, for example:

- donation of equipment or materials (copying machines, paper, pencils, etc.);
- making someone on its staff available for a period of time during the day;
- donating its expertise—the accounts department of a corporation, for example, may examine the administrative and management makeup of an organization and recommend ways to increase efficiency;
- agreeing to subsidize day care costs (in the case that you are a day care center) of employees who send their children to the center.

Determine the corporate motivation for giving. The tax breaks corporations are entitled to by the IRS do not mean very much to corporations. What is meaningful to them, however, includes the following:

1. the public relations aspect of the charitable donation, as was demonstrated by the Ohio fast-food chain event; and
2. the appeal to their needs and the benefit the contribution is likely to have for their employees.

Appeal to corporate needs

Firms dealing with engineering equipment are more likely to make significant contributions to engineering departments in universities than they are to programs for the handicapped, simply because they see this type of contribution as an investment in the future of their business. With regard to corporate giving within a particular field, nonprofit institutions seeking corporate funds should:

1. Locate those corporations that have some relevance to the grant-seeking organization. In the case of early childhood programs,

these may be children's clothes manufacturers, toy manufacturers, fast-food chains, etc. Those organizations serving families may consider approaching large discount stores.

2. Have the answer to one basic question before approaching the corporation: What are the benefits to the corporation that supports your organization? Would one be that many of the clients you serve are their employees? Or their customers? Could the corporation derive publicity from the event? If so, how?

Foundations

Foundations make grants totalling more than $2 billion a year. It is not surprising then that many nonprofit organizations are looking for foundations to replace government funds. When seeking to use foundations as a source of support, however, some realism is in order. While 1980 figures show that foundations' combined assets have climbed to above $41 billion (American Association of Fund Raising Counsel, Inc. 1981), inflation has actually reduced the purchasing power of their holdings by 30 percent over the last seven years. In addition, the requests for assistance submitted to foundations have soared. Some foundation executives estimate that the number of requests has risen by 30 percent; others contend that it has doubled. During the next few years the number of organizations seeking foundation support will continue to increase.

In order to successfully solicit foundation support, it is necessary to be thoroughly familiar with types and background of foundations and some of the basic principles of foundation grant seeking. These should serve you not as absolute rules, for there are none, but as guidelines for learning on your own what is the most successful approach.

Foundations account for a small share of the money contributed by the private sector. The bulk of the money, as noted earlier, is contributed by living individuals, who account for some 75 percent of the contributions, and through bequests about 14 percent.

Foundations' activities were largely ignored by law makers until 1969, when Congress enacted the Tax Reform Act. Since then, foundations have been required to operate under a strict set of laws. Subject to the laws, foundations must now pay excise tax on their investment income; distribute in grants a specified percentage of their assets each year; submit detailed reports on how the grants are being used; own no more than 20 percent of any corporation's voting shares; and make no investments that would endanger their assets.

The results of the Tax Reform Act of 1969 and its subsequent revisions have been to the benefit of grant seekers. The required reporting procedures allow anyone to have access to data on foundation giving, and there is an increased professionalism and sense of accountability among the managers of foundations.

Identify an appropriate foundation

There are more than 23,000 grant-making foundations in the United States. Most of them are very small and many are administered by a bank for very specific purposes. There are different types of foundations. Knowing how they differ will help the potential grant seeker choose the appropriate foundation to approach.

General purpose foundations. These are usually the big foundations. Among the best known are the Ford Foundation, the Rockefeller Foundation, and the Carnegie Corporation. General purpose foundations are also referred to as independent foundations because they are not influenced by the donor or family. Although there are only about 400 such foundations, they are responsible for giving away well over half of all foundation grants.

Most general purpose foundations have broad based grant-making policies and enjoy supporting innovative projects with far reaching effects. The average size of their individual grant is quite large; $500,000 or multimillion dollar awards are not uncommon. They have full-time administrative staffs and prestigious boards of trustees.

Company foundations. These are also known as corporate foundations, or flow-through foundations, in that they are sponsored by the company bearing their name. Among the better known company foundations are the Alcoa Foundation, the Sears Roebuck Foundation, and the United States Steel Foundation. Although company foundations are legally independent of their company sponsors, they sometimes share the same governing boards, and most tend to fund causes closely related to their company's financial interests and employees' interests. Some such foundations have assets of their own. Many others distribute funds channeled to them by the sponsoring company (hence the term flow-through).

Community foundations. There are approximately 200 community foundations in the United States. Each is local in scope, restricted to distributing funds within the community and governed by prominent local citizens. Community foundations usually receive money from many local sources, manage the money, and distribute it according to the wishes of the donor(s). The largest community foundation is the Cleveland Foundation with assets exceeding $100 million. Because the amount of funds community foundations have to allocate for specific causes may be limited, many prefer to provide seed money so that programs can be initiated and later funded by other sources.

Family foundations. This is by far the largest category of foundations, with more than 20,000 such foundations in existence. However, they control only about 15 percent of total foundation assets. Most of these foundations were founded by a wealthy individual or family to distribute money according to the donor's wishes. They rarely have permanent staff; administrative duties are usually handled on a part-time basis or by the donor's family. They are thus less formal in their operation and at times more receptive to a personal approach from grant seekers.

Special purpose foundations. These foundations were usually founded by a will or a trust to give money to one specific cause or locality. Generally, their grant-making policies are narrowly defined, such as "to help families of merchant seamen." However, some fund broader causes such as education and leadership. Unlike grant-making policies of the foundations in the other categories, these special purpose foundations are not likely to change over time.

Private foundations differ in size, geographical limitations, staff, funding policies, and in one other characteristic: whether they are known as operating or nonoperating foundations. Operating foundations generally undertake their own projects. An example is the Menninger Foundation which is a psychiatric institute providing service and research. They generally do not fund projects outside their own organization.

Rejection rates for proposals sent to foundations are generally not available, but estimates range between 90 percent and 95 percent. Many rejected proposals are worth funding but unfortunately are submitted to inappropriate foundations. Before approaching any foundation with a request for a grant, it is important to do extensive research to find answers to the following questions.

1. Does the program to be funded fall under the foundation's funding policy?
2. Is the organization to be funded within the geographical parameters established by the foundation (if there are any)?
3. Is the amount of money requested within the range of average grants made by the foundation?
4. Does the foundation have any restrictions on what it will fund? Some foundations do not fund equipment or salary of personnel, for example, so while the organization may require total funding for a program, a request for partial funding may be in order.

How to research foundations. To find out answers to the above, background research is necessary. The first source to look for is the *Foundation Directory*, available in the reference section of most public libraries. It is published every two years, so the information compiled in the *Directory* is not necessarily up to date and will need to be verified.

The *Directory* includes an alphabetical listing of all foundations by *states*. Information provided for each foundation includes the name and address of the foundation, year of incorporation, donor(s), financial data (assets, grants made in a year, average amount of grant), trustees and staff members, name of person to contact, and type of inquiries accepted. Some listings also include any funding restrictions.

There are other indexes in the *Directory*, including one on *field of interest*, so those interested in early childhood education, for example, can compile a list of all foundations which in the past funded that area. Studying the *Foundation Directory* will produce a broad list of possible foundations to approach.

Similar information is also available from other sources, including the *Foundation Grants Index*, or through a computerized search, both of which are available at the Foundation Center in New York or at one of the regional Foundation Centers (see Bibliography). Many universities also include the *Foundation Grants Index* in the libraries of their development offices. Staff members at these offices often allow others in the community to make use of their resources. The *Index* is an annual reference book that includes lists and cross-references of nearly 10,000 grants of $5,000 or more reported from 250 major foundations. The three indexes included are subject (area of interest), recipient, and foundation.

The list of foundations generated by the preliminary research should be narrowed down to about five. This is achieved by updating the information and verifying whether or not a particular foundation meets the needs of the organization seeking funds. More current information on the type of foundation and its grant-making policies is available in annual reports, or on Internal Revenue Service (IRS) Forms 999 and 990AR, which foundations are required to submit annually. Microfilmed copies of the completed forms are available at the Foundation Centers. If time permits, more information can be sought by calling the foundation staff, or requesting information to be sent by mail. Many foundations may refuse to oblige callers, but others would be happy to send their annual reports.

Most foundation managers state that they prefer that an initial contact be made by letter. If this is the case, a letter explaining the nature of the applicant organization, the amount of money desired, and for what purpose, should be sent. If there is interest in funding, the foundation staff would indicate follow-up procedures, including guidelines for submitting a proposal. Although it is extremely difficult to do, the serious contender for foundation funds should attempt to make a personal contact with someone (preferably the executive director) on the staff.

Final decisions on funding are made by the foundation's board of directors. Foundation boards meet at least once a year, with many meeting as often as four times a year. In order to consider proposals at these meetings, each foundation has a deadline, or a series of deadlines, for submitting proposals. As a general rule, proposals should be ready to submit in December (the end of foundations' fiscal year) or some time during the winter months for consideration in the spring. A good time to begin the research on foundations is during the summer when most foundation staff are vacationing. In this way, personal contact can be made in the early fall, followed by writing and submission of proposals during the late winter or fall.

Implications for your organization

Having some knowledge of the background of foundations in America, what kinds of foundations there are, and the type of research you need to do in order to acquire more information, you will need to remember the following:

1. There are no general rules in applying for a foundation grant. Many books listed in the Bibliography can provide you with the basic principles of the research and the approach, but it is up to you to find out what works for you and with what foundation.
2. Request an explanation for a rejection. Once you approach a foundation and submit a grant proposal, it is up to you to ask foundation staff to explain to you clearly and precisely why you were turned down. This information will be useful to you in soliciting funds from other foundations as well as knowing better the foundation which rejected your application.
3. Even if you are rejected, write a letter to the foundation staff thanking them for their time and effort and expressing the hope that you can work with them at a later date.
4. Nurture foundations. Send regular reports on what is happening in your organization, photographs, newsletters, and any other literature to foundations that support your program. Or, invite the foundation staff for an informal visit. Include foundations which rejected your application on your mailing list, so that if you approach them in following years, your organization may then be familiar to them.

Government

In this book we de-emphasize government support of children's services in favor of other options for funding. It is important that programs move away from dependence on the government grant. It is equally important, however, that we not entirely give up on the public sector but instead forge new and different relationships with government.

This is important for two reasons. First, decisions which affect children and families will continue to be made, as will the identification of national and local priorities—which programs will be eliminated, which will receive substantial budget cuts, and which will remain relatively intact. Whether you are going to continue to depend on government funds for your individual program or find new sources of support, you should keep a stake in the policy process, and you should try to influence legislation to support the children's cause.

Related to this is the second reason why you should not give up on the public sector, which is that some public money will still be available, although at this writing it will be channeled primarily through the states in block grants. It is up to you to see that your program is not eliminated and that you stay afloat through the aid of public support until you find other means of raising money.

Working with state and local government

States are assuming their new authority over a broad range of social services. Within each state, social services programs are likely to be thrown into competition with each other for a portion of the block grant. What are the chances for your program's continuation? You may find that your best policy route is to coalesce with other early childhood programs and to work together to see that children's services get their fair share.

Here are some ways you should work with government either as a member of a coalition or as an individual:

1. Become involved in political debates and keep abreast of other advocacy concerns such as housing, the elderly, and public assistance. Your ability to tie children's issues into these debates will work to ensure that children's needs are not overlooked.
2. Get to know state and local officials and individuals and collectively approach them to speak on children's needs.
3. Become involved in state and local political campaigns; help promote candidates in your area.

4. Broaden your base of support. Seek others in the community to help you champion the children's cause. These may be parents in your program. Each parent, for example, may be asked to seek five friends or co-workers to help in some way—to send letters to legislators, to attend meetings, to help write proposals, etc.

Making the presentation

Presenting your case to a potential donor, be that an individual, corporation, foundation, or government agency, is likely to be your most important move. Whether or not you receive a pledge for support or a grant, and in what amount, will depend in large part on how well you promote your cause and your organization. The approach to soliciting individuals is discussed in the previous chapter. In this section, the emphasis is on making the presentation to corporate and foundation executives.

Initiate contacts

There are two ways to make an initial presentation: in person, if it is possible, or by letter. Personal contact is by far the most effective approach. It enables you to know the corporation or foundation staff more intimately, and it enables them to have a sense of who you are and what type of organization you represent. They will be more likely to remember organizations with whom they have had personal contact. The initial presentation will no doubt be followed by a proposal for funding which you can either leave with the potential supporter or send at a later date.

Whether the initial presentation is in person or through a letter, your task is to convey information about your organization. The use of printed material and visual aids will greatly facilitate the presentation and will enhance others' understanding of your organization. Here is a list of materials you may consider taking with you to the presentation, or enclosing in an initial letter:

■ detailed budget;
■ list of current sources of funding;

■ organizational chart, i.e., duties and responsibilities of board members and personnel;

■ biographical information on board members;

■ description of physical facilities;

■ description of clientele served;

■ the impact of the program on your clients and the community; here you can include the history of the program, success stories, copies of newspaper articles, etc.;

■ letters of support from experts in the field, other community agencies who are aware of your program, parents, etc.

Write the proposal

Many service providers have very good ideas about the kinds of programs they want to offer their clients and, when money is available, they are well versed at implementing their ideas. However, the reality is that in many cases, for example with foundation support, the idea has to be translated into a project, on paper, before the money becomes available, and this has to be done well. In other words, the entire project has to be conceptualized and then presented in the form of a proposal to a funding source.

Federal and state governments, foundations, and/or corporations warrant different proposals, depending on their guidelines. As a general rule, however, it must be remembered that, after the initial presentation, a grant proposal is the second most important phase in the quest for support. Its components should reflect all requirements of the specific funding agency and should be strongly interrelated so that there is a flow from beginning to end.

Grant proposals are usually long. They present a reading task for the reviewer. If the reviewer can easily read and understand the proposal, she or he is more likely to be impressed with its contents and more inclined to honor the request for funds. A grant proposal must address the following questions: *what, why, how, who, where, when.* These are the general questions that a journalist answers in a news story, but the order in which they appear here is particular to grant writing. In addition to these, two other questions must be addressed in the proposal: *how long*—the duration of the proposed project; and *how well*—the evaluation component built into the proposal.

Guidelines for proposals vary, and it is very important to abide by the guidelines specified and to include all the information requested by the funding source. Generally, a proposal includes the following elements:

1. *Summary/abstract.* This précis encompasses the entire proposal and is usually not longer than one page.

2. *Purpose of and need for the program.* This section includes specific statements about the purpose of the program and why the program is deemed important. Using data to determine the need is essential.

3. *Goal and objectives.* A goal is a single statement indicating the extent and characteristics of accomplishments to be achieved. It should be related to the purpose/need.

    Objectives are the specific steps that must be carried out in order to achieve the goal. If the goal of the project is to enhance the mental health of children in a day care center, then the objectives may be to: (a) provide weekly child counseling sessions; (b) provide parent workshops on children's needs; (c) provide reading materials related to specific problems children have, etc. It is very important at this stage to be realistic about how much can be accomplished given the time and the amount of money requested. (See Appendix B for examples.)

4. *Methodology/narrative.* Directly related to the goal and objectives, this section is a detailed description of what is to be accomplished and how. A description of the activities to be undertaken, the timelines (see Appendix C) for their accomplishment, indications of who will be responsible for carrying out activities, job descriptions, etc., are included in this section.

5. *Budget.* This part is often placed at the beginning of the proposal, for it is the first item the funding source is interested in. It is the most closely scrutinized aspect of the proposal. Care should be taken to include in the budget everything that is referred to in the text of the proposal, and vice versa. For example, if a program for a mobile rural area teacher training program includes mention of a van to be used to transport materials, the cost of buying the vehicle and its maintenance (including mileage) should be reflected in the

et. Something like this can easily be forgotten, especially if a van, for example, is already available to a program and money is not requested for it. In cases such as this, it is important to have two columns in the budget, one for amount requested and the other for in-kind contributions. A third column, funds to be requested from other sources, can be added if the amount requested from the funding source represents only partial support. In this way the reader is given a realistic representation of the costs involved.

It is equally easy to make the mistake of including in the budget items such as travel or office supplies without having mentioned these in the text. What will the travel money be used for? Before submitting a proposal to a funding agency, it is wise to read it one more time with special attention paid to all the items included in the budget to see that they are also included in the text, and vice versa.

6. *Evaluation.* It is important for the funding agency to have a sense that the applicant is responsible, accountable, and committed to evaluation of the program. Assessing how well the project is doing, its impact and acceptance in the community, should be important to the applicant also. An evaluation plan, including the process of the evaluation, who will do the evaluation, the time at which the evaluation will be conducted, and when and to whom the evaluation will be reported, should be included.

7. *Appendixes.* The proposal should be easy to read. Any items that are helpful but that would distract from the flow should be appended. This would include information on the applicant organization (board composition; a letter from the Internal Revenue Service stating that your organization has qualified as a tax-exempt organization under section 501(c)(3) of the IRS Code; other programs provided, etc.); assurances (in the case of federal grants); and letters of support—these are very important and should be included whether or not they are requested. It is very gratifying to the funding agency to know the status of the applicant organization and to have a sense of its credibility in the community.

A cover letter from the chief executive of the applicant organization should be brief and should include mention of the total amount of funds requested.

Proofread the proposal

The staff of the National Endowment for the Humanities compiled a list of seven frequent errors found in proposals which were rejected. Make sure your proposal has been carefully written, and proofread it after the final typing to avoid these errors.

1. The budget does not relate closely to the activities described in the narrative.
2. The application does not provide all information requested, including complete identification of personnel for the project and their qualifications for the assignment.
3. The application is marred by inflated rhetoric and ignorance of similar projects.
4. Arguments in support of the application are subjective and unconvincing—applicant assumes reader is familiar with or disposed to support the application.
5. The plan of work is missing or is too vague. The application shows disorganization of proposed activities and illogical ordering of specific tasks.
6. The application is distorted by errors in grammar, fact, spelling, and mathematics, or the application is sloppy (missing pages and cited attachments, unreadable copies).
7. The application does not give adequate attention to dissemination/distribution of the products of the projects.

Follow-up

Proposal writing is hard work, especially because the amount of time available to execute the product is usually too short. A sense of relief accompanies the final stage of submitting the proposal. But the work is not over at that point.

If the proposal is funded, letters of thanks to the funding agency and all those who participated in the execution of the proposal are warranted. As soon as possible, the stage must be set for implementing the program. Once the program is underway, it is advisable to maintain contact with the funding agency, to nurture its staff. Include it on mailing lists, if there are any; advise of the program to date; and invite participation of its staff members. Contact should be maintained as a matter of courtesy and will prove important for future requests for funding.

If the proposal is rejected, it is imperative to find out why. This is often due to the competition, in which case other funding sources should be identified and the proposal recycled accordingly. In the case of federal and state grants, comments of readers (those at the agency who review the proposals) should be requested and analyzed. Foundations and corporations usually indicate why, in general terms, the proposal is rejected. If the reasons given are general in nature, you should request more specific information either by letter or telephone. A rejection should be followed up with a letter of thanks to the funding agency staff for their time and effort in the consideration of the proposal, and it should express the hope that future proposals will be considered.

Fundraising: costs and responsibilities 6

It costs money to raise money. The amount of money your organization will be able to allocate for fundraising and the number of volunteer supporters you have will therefore determine the fundraising method(s) to be chosen, and the scale on which the method(s) are implemented. The main items of a fundraising budget are

- salaries or percentage of time, donated help, etc., for a director/fundraising coordinator and staff
- secretarial costs, salary and supplies, including telephone
- printing costs for the preparation of informative literature, publicity, etc.
- travel/transportation allowances for meeting with potential donors
- miscellaneous costs, depending on the method employed: renting lists of potential donors, postage, entertainment, legal fees, auditors' fees, fundraising counsel, feasibility studies, etc.

Who is responsible for fundraising?

Large philanthropic organizations have not one but several employees who are responsible for different fundraising efforts. They are usually answerable to the organization's director of development, or its president. In smaller organizations, the task of fundraising is often one of the responsibilities of the executive director who also has to oversee the entire operation of the organization. Who will be responsible for fundraising in your organization will depend on the organizational structure of your program and the amount of money you have available for fundraising.

Options for fundraising responsibility include the following:

1. You may commit a percentage of your time to fundraising.
2. You may solicit the help of your staff in carrying out some of the details involved.
3. You may solicit the help of volunteers.
4. You may hire professional fundraising consultants.

The first two options require no further explanation other than that you need to be aware of the limitations involved, depending on the amount of time you and your staff have. But there are some points to be made with regard to the use of volunteers or professional consultants.

The role of volunteers

The advantages for using volunteers in fundraising efforts are listed below:

1. It is a good way of cultivating prospects and soliciting potential donors. Also, volunteers themselves are potential donors.
2. It is a good way to increase your organization's visibility and credibility in the community.
3. Most importantly, it is a good way for you to get help in carrying out details, especially if you are short of money and do not have sufficient time to do the work yourself.

There are some disadvantages in using volunteers. For example, they may not like to take orders, they may be good only at simple tasks, they may carry out the task too slowly or without enthusiasm, etc. When you know these factors, however, you may prevent problems by having volunteers work under supervision, by making the tasks more enjoyable through promoting work parties, or by assigning only short-term or simple tasks to volunteers.

The new volunteers

The other problem with volunteers may be the difficulty you may encounter in finding them. Housewives made up a large portion of

America's volunteer corps for many years. They were the backbone of innumerable charitable campaigns and were counted upon for their services in hospitals, religious organizations, community groups, and educational agencies. Many women, of course, still continue this tradition. However, as more and more women join the work force as full-time paid workers, the supply of volunteers is diminishing. Given this fact, there are certain changes that could be made in order to solicit the help of volunteers:

1. Change your image of the traditional volunteer. In the mid-Seventies there were close to 37 million volunteers in America (United States Government Census Bureau 1974). Forty-two percent of them were between the ages of 25 and 44, and only 8 percent were retirees. The concept of the new volunteer should include not only women and men between 25 and 44, but also more retirees and younger people, such as high school students.

2. Adjust your schedule to accommodate the new volunteers' available time. Retirees may be able to work during the day, but working women and men may only be able to volunteer during the evenings and weekends, and they may need short assignments rather than continuing responsibilities.

3. Change the approach to soliciting the help of volunteers. Rather than contacting individuals, why not contact large groups or corporations? You may approach, for example
   - a rest home director who may inquire about retirees' interest in helping on a project
   - a high school teacher who may be willing to commit the class to a project involving helping your organization
   - a corporation which has among its employee benefits the provision of employee leaves of absence for a period of several months, with pay, to do volunteer work in the community
   - a corporation which may, as a token of its support, provide you with the expertise available within its organization for several hours per week or for a certain period of time to complete a specific project, such as developing informational literature about your program

Professional fundraising counsel

Established nonprofit organizations have professional fundraisers on their staff, or they hire executive directors with proven track records in fundraising. Often, such organizations hire additional fundraising consultants to train the staff in a specific fundraising effort, increase the odds of success of a fundraising event, or conduct a feasibility study. Options for hiring fundraising consultants vary from hiring one consultant on a one-day-per-week basis to employing large fundraising management or public relations firms.

Should your organization hire a fundraising consultant/firm?

As you ponder this question, consider the following advantages to bringing in outside experts.

1. They can provide an experienced and objective point of view concerning your organization's potential for fundraising.
2. They can stimulate you and your staff to develop a continuing and active development program.

You must remember, however, that no matter how reputable or experienced the consultants

- they are not equipped with a magic formula for success
- they cannot do the job entirely by themselves
- they need cooperation from you, your staff, and your board

You must also consider the costs involved and be sure to hire only ethical and reputable prople. The National Society for Fund Raising Executives (NSFRE) is currently completing a certification procedure for professionals in the field. Once instituted, certification will be open to fundraisers who have worked full time in the field for a minimum of five years. Through a program of education and testing, these individuals will be certified to insure that they possess the knowledge of theory and technique that should be expected of professional fundraisers. Those certified will have to pledge in writing that their fundraising activities will be conducted in accordance with the NSFRE Code of Ethics and Professional Practices, and will be entitled to use *C.F.R.E.* (Certified Fund Raising Executive) after their names.

Feasibility study

The costs of some fundraising methods, and the effort involved, can become quite extensive. This is especially true in the case of annual and capital campaigns, direct mail solicitations, and certain special event activities. Once your organization is able to allocate enough money toward fundraising costs to warrant conducting these events, you may consider doing a feasibility study.

A feasibility study is a survey which determines whether the organization is ready for the particular fundraising event, whether the community would support the event, and where the funds are likely to come from. Beyond determining whether the organization should go ahead with its fundraising plans and its potential for development, the feasibility study is important in several other respects.

1. It points to the strengths and weaknesses of the organization.
2. It identifies potential donors and sources of support and leadership.
3. It establishes a framework for long-range planning.

A feasibility study should not be conducted by the organization's own staff, but by an outside evaluation team, if it is to be objective and accurate. Depending on your organizational framework, past experience in fundraising, and the availability of data, the costs for such an effort may be $5,000 or more.

Professional fundraising and management firms, or professional fundraising consultants may be hired to conduct the feasibility study. Banks may also be of assistance. For example, the Hartford (Connecticut) National Bank provides nonprofit organizations in Connecticut and western Massachusetts with a detailed planning questionnaire. The questionnaire is completed by the organization and analyzed by a team of experts.

*   *   *

Conclusion

There are many ways to raise money for philanthropic causes. Most of these require imagination, research, the willingness to work, and persistence. The growth and development of many fine nonprofit humanitarian organizations in America is attributable to the professionalism, knowledge, and dedication of their leaders and supporters.

With the same techniques, services for young children and their families also can thrive. With some imagination, a lot of research, hard work, and persistence, programs for low-income, handicapped, and gifted children can continue to operate, and child care, early childhood education, and parent support services can become independent and established.

This book is intended to trigger within each of you the desire to investigate options for funding that go beyond the public sector. If only one of the examples stimulates you to initiate a fundraising activity or to plan a course of action, this goal will have been achieved.

References

Annual Survey of Corporate Contributions, 1981. Available from The Conference Board, 845 Third Ave., New York, NY 10022.

Bromberg, R. S. "Tax Problems of Daycare Centers." *Philanthropy Monthly* 12, no 1 (1979): 18–21.

Fund Raising Practices of United Way Agencies in N.Y. City. November 1980. Available from Greater New York Fund/United Way, 99 Park Ave., New York, NY 10016. Also reviewed in *Philanthropy Monthly*, December 1980.

Giving USA. 1981 edition. Published annually by the American Association of Fund Raising Counsel, Inc., 25 W. 43rd St., New York, NY 10036.

Standard and Poor's Register of Corporations, Directors and Executives. 3 vols. Standard and Poor's Corporation, 25 Broadway, New York, NY 10004. Published annually.

Statistical Abstracts of the United States Government Census Bureau. Washington, D.C.: United States Government Census Bureau, 1974.

Who's Who in America. Chicago: Marquis Who's Who. Published annually.

Who's Who in Finance and Industry. Chicago: Marquis Who's Who, 1974–75.

Bibliography

Reference books

Giving USA. American Association of Fund Raising Counsel, Inc., 25 W. 43rd St., New York, NY 10036. Published annually.

Gross, M., and Warshauer, W. *Financial and Accounting Guide for Non-Profit Organizations*, 3rd ed. New York: Wiley, 1979.

Law-Yone, W. *Company Information: A Model Investigation.* Washington, D.C.: Washington Researchers, 1980.

Standard and Poor's Register of Corporations, Directors and Executives. 3 vols. Standard and Poor's Corporation, 25 Broadway, New York, NY 10004. Published annually.

Survey of State Laws Regulating Charitable Solicitations. Annual subscription service. Ed. J. J. Stevenson. *The Philanthropy Monthly,* Box 989, New Milford, CT 06776.

Taft Corporate Information System. Directory published annually and newsletter published monthly. Taft Corporation, 5125 MacArthur Blvd., N.W., Washington, DC 20016.

The Taft Trustees of Wealth. 1979–80. Taft Corporation, 5125 MacArthur Blvd., N.W., Washington, DC 20016.

Who's Who in America. Chicago: Marquis Who's Who. Published annually.

Who's Who in Finance and Industry. Chicago: Marquis Who's Who, 1974–75.

Zaltman, G. *Management Principles of Non-Profit Agencies.* 1981. Public Service Materials Center, 111 N. Central Ave., Hartsdale, NY 10530.

Other reference material

Clotfeller, C.T., and Salamon, L. M. "The Federal Government and the Nonprofit Sector: The Impact of the 1981 Tax Act on Individual Charitable Giving. A Study for the Independent Sector." 1981. The Urban Institute, 2100 M St., N.W., Washington, DC 20037.

Fund Raising Practices of United Way Agencies in New York City. November, 1980. Prepared by the Nova Institute for the Greater New York Fund/United Way, 99 Park Ave., New York, NY 10016.

Fundraising manuals

Gurin, M. G. *What Volunteers Should Know for Successful Fund Raising.* New York: Stein and Day, 1981.

Manual of Practical Fund Raising. 1975. Massachusetts VITA, 294 Washington St., Boston, MA 02108.

Pendleton, N. *Fund Raising: A Guide for Non-Profit Organizations.* Englewood Cliffs, N.J.: Prentice-Hall, 1981.

Taylor, B. P. *Guide to Successful Fund Raising.* 2nd ed. South Plainfield, N.J.: Groupwork Today, Inc., 1981.

Warner, I. R. *The Art of Fund Raising.* New York: Harper & Row, 1975.

Corporate giving

Fremont-Smith, M. R. *Philanthropy and the Business Corporation.* New York: Russell Sage Foundation, 1972.

Hillman, H. *The Art of Winning Corporate Grants.* New York: Vanguard Press, 1979.

Profiles of Involvement: The Handbook of Corporate Social Responsibility. The Human Resources Network, 2010 Chancellor St., Philadelphia, PA 19103.

Foundations

Dermer, J. *Where America's Large Foundations Make Their Grants.* 1980–81. Public Service Materials Center, 355 Lexington Ave., New York, NY 10017.

Dermer, J. *The New How to Raise Funds from Foundations.* 1975. Public Service Materials Center, 355 Lexington Ave., New York, NY 10017.

Dermer, J. *How to Write Successful Foundation Presentations.* 1975. Public Service Materials Center, 355 Lexington Ave., New York, NY 10017.

Heimann, F. R., ed. *The Future of Foundations.* 1973. Distributed by Prentice-Hall, Englewood Cliffs, N.J.

Hillman, H., and Abarbanel, K. *The Art of Winning Foundation Grants.* New York: Vanguard Press, 1975.

Kurzig, C. M. *Foundation Fundamentals: A Guide for Grantseekers.* 1980. Available from The Foundation Center, 888 Seventh Ave., New York, NY 10019.

Richman, S. *Public Information Handbook for Foundations.* New York: Council on Foundations, 1973.

Taft, J. R. *Understanding Foundations.* New York: McGraw-Hill, 1967.

Zurcher, A. J. *Management of America's Foundations: Administration, Policies and Social Role.* New York: New York University Press, 1972.

Zurcher, A. J., and Dustan, J. *The Foundation Administrator: A Study of Those Who Manage America's Foundations.* New York: Russell Sage Foundation, 1972.

Proposal writing

Crawford, J., and Kielsmeier, C. *Proposal Writing.* Available from Continuing Education Publications, Waldo 100, Corvallis, OR 97331.

Kiritz, N. J. *Program Planning and Proposal Writing.* Available from The Grantsmanship Center, 1015 W. Olympic Blvd., Los Angeles, CA 90015.

Lefferts, R. *Getting a Grant: How to Write Successful Grant Proposals.* Englewood Cliffs, N.J.: Prentice-Hall, 1978.

White, V. P. *Grants: How to Find Out about Them and What to Do Next.* New York: Plenum, 1975.

Periodicals and newsletters

Foundation News. Council on Foundations, 1828 L St., N.W., Washington, DC 20506. This publication includes news on foundation activities and people in the field as well as an index of current projects funded by foundations, including foundation name and address, amount, and purpose of the grant offered.

FRI Newsletter. The Fund Raising Institute, Box 365, Ambler, PA 19002. Provides current information on fundraising practices and developments.

Fund Raising Management. Hoke Communications, Inc., 224 Seventh St., Garden City, NY 11530. Provides information and news on fundraising activities.

Grantsmanship Center News. The Grantsmanship Center, 650 S. Spring St., Suite 507, Los Angeles, CA 90014. This publication includes important how-to tips and reports on grant-making activities.

LRC Newsbriefs. Lutheran Resources Commission, 5 Thomas Circle, N.W., Washington, DC 20005. One of the best sources of information on grants available for application from a variety of sources. Presented according to categories which include children and education.

The Philanthropy Monthly. Box 989, New Milford, CT 06776. This professional publication is read by foundation executives, corporate contributions officers, executives of nonprofit organizations, and lawyers and accountants representing nonprofit organizations. It includes current and comprehensive reviews on developments in fundraising and research on foundation/corporate grantmaking patterns and news of events in the foundation and fundraising field.

Services

The Grantsmanship Center
650 S. Spring St., Suite 507
Los Angeles, CA 90014
213-689-9222
Conducts week-long training sessions on fundraising and grants administration; publishes *The Grantsmanship Center News,* which contains reports on federal and foundation grant patterns.

Taft Information System
Taft Corporation
5125 MacArthur Blvd., N.W.
Washington, DC 20016
202-966-7086
Provides fundraising research and consultation services and publishes several research tools such as foundation and corporate directories.

The Foundation Center
(national and regional locations; for addresses, see below)
The Foundation Center is a central clearinghouse for materials related to foundations. The Center includes among its activities publications and other services.

Publications of The Foundation Center

These and other publications are available for use at The Foundation Center Library in New York or at the regional centers (for addresses, see end of this section). These publications are also available in other libraries and may be purchased.

Foundation Directory, containing information on over 2,000 of the largest foundations in the United States. It is cross-indexed according to subject, state or city, trustees and administrators, foundation donors, and foundation names.

The Foundation Grants Index is a compilation of the Grants Index supplement published in *Foundation News*. It provides a detailed summary of grants awarded by major foundations.

Foundation Grants to Individuals describes programs/policies of foundations that make grants to individuals.

Foundation Center National Data Book is a directory which includes information on all foundations in the United States. It is indexed alphabetically and by state and provides basic information such as address of the foundation, its officers, contact person, assets, and average amount of the grants made.

Foundation News is a bimonthly magazine featuring news and articles on developments in the foundation field.

Services of The Foundation Center

These services are available on an annual fee-for-membership basis.

The Comsearch Printouts is a computer service which provides information on foundations.

The Associate Program offers customized information on foundations.

Centerline is a toll-free telephone reference service.

Centerline News is a series of taped bulletins on foundation news. Available each week via WATS line.

Locations of The Foundation Center

Alabama

Birmingham Public Library
2100 Park Place
Birmingham 35203
205-226-3600

Huntsville-Madison County Public
Library
108 Fountain Circle
P.O. Box 443
Huntsville 35804
205-532-5940

University of South Alabama
Library Building
Reference Department
Mobile 36688
205-460-7025

Auburn University at Montgomery
Library
Montgomery 36193-0401
205-271-9649

Alaska

University of Alaska,
Anchorage Library
3211 Providence Drive
Anchorage 99508
907-786-1848

Arizona

Phoenix Public Library Business and
Sciences Department
12 East McDowell Road
Phoenix 85004
602-262-4636

Tucson Public Library
Main Library
200 South Sixth Avenue
Tucson 85701
602-791-4393

The Foundation Center*
312 Sutter Street, Room 312
San Francisco 94108
415-397-0902

Grantsmanship Resource Center
Junior League of San Jose, Inc.
Community Foundation of Santa Clara
County
960 West Hedding, Suite 220
San Jose 95126
408-244-5280

Orange County Community
Developmental Council
1440 East First Street, 4th Floor
Santa Ana 92701
714-547-6801

Peninsula Community Foundation
1204 Burlingame Avenue
Burlingame 94011-0627
415-342-2505

Santa Barbara Public Library
Reference Section
40 East Anapamu
P.O. Box 1019
Santa Barbara 93102
805-962-7653

Santa Monica Public Library
1343 Sixth Street
Santa Monica 90401-1603
213-458-8603

Tuolomne County Library
465 S. Washington Street
Sonora 95370
209-533-5707

District of Columbia

The Foundation Center**
1001 Connecticut Avenue, NW
Washington 20036
202-331-1400

Florida

Volusia County Public Library
City Island
Daytona Beach 32014
904-252-8374

Jacksonville Public Library
Business, Science, and Industry
Department
122 North Ocean Street
Jacksonville 32202
904-633-3926

Miami-Dade Public Library
Humanities Department
101 W. Flagler St.
Miami 33132
305-375-2665

Orlando Public Library
101 E. Central Blvd.
Orlando 32801
305-425-4694

Selby Public Library
1001 Boulevard of the Arts
Sarasota 33577
813-366-7303

Leon County Public Library
Community Funding Resources Center
1940 North Monroe Street
Tallahassee 32303
904-478-2665

Donors Forum of Chicago
53 W. Jackson Blvd., Rm. 430
Chicago 60604
312-431-0265

Evanston Public Library
1703 Orrington Avenue
Evanston 60201
312-866-0305

Sangamon State University Library
Shepherd Road
Springfield 62708
217-786-6633

Indiana

Allen County Public Library
900 Webster Street
Fort Wayne 46802
219-424-7241

Indiana University Northwest Library
3400 Broadway
Gary 46408
219-980-6580

Indianapolis-Marion County Public
Library
40 East St. Clair Street
Indianapolis 46204
317-269-1733

Iowa

Public Library of Des Moines
100 Locust Street
Des Moines 50308
515-283-4259

Kansas

Topeka Public Library
Adult Services Department
1515 West Tenth Street
Topeka 66604
913-233-2040

Arkansas

Westark Community College Library
Grand Avenue at Waldron Road
Fort Smith 72913
501-785-7000

Little Rock Public Library
Reference Department
700 Louisiana Street
Little Rock 72201
501-370-5950

California

California Community Foundation
Funding Information Center
3580 Wilshire Blvd., Suite 1660
Los Angeles 90010
213-413-4042

Community Foundation for Monterey County
420 Pacific Street
Monterey 93940
408-375-9712

California Community Foundation
4050 Metropolitan Drive #300
Orange 92668
714-937-9077

Riverside Public Library
3581 7th Street
Riverside 92501
714-782-5201

California State Library
Reference Services, Rm. 309
914 Capital Mall
Sacramento 95814
916-322-4570

San Diego Community Foundation
525 "B" Street, Suite 410
San Diego 92101
619-239-8815

Colorado

Pikes Peak Library District
20 North Cascade Avenue
Colorado Springs 80901
303-473-2780

Denver Public Library
Sociology Division
1357 Broadway
Denver 80203
303-571-2190

Connecticut

Danbury Public Library
170 Main Street
Danbury 06810
203-797-4527

Hartford Public Library
Reference Department
500 Main Street
Hartford 06103
203-525-9121

D.A.T.A.
30 Arbor Street
Hartford 06106
203-232-6619

D.A.T.A.
25 Science Park
Suite 502
New Haven 06511
203-786-5225

Delaware

Hugh Morris Library
University of Delaware
Newark 19717-5267
302-451-2965

Wichita Public Library
223 South Main
Wichita 67202
316-262-0611

Kentucky

Western Kentucky University
Division of Library Services
Helm-Cravens Library
Bowling Green 42101
502-745-3951

Louisville Free Public Library
Fourth and York Streets
Louisville 40203
502-561-8600

Palm Beach County Community Foundation
324 Datura Street, Suite 340
West Palm Beach 33401
305-659-6800

Georgia

Atlanta-Fulton Public Library
Ivan Allen Department
1 Margaret Mitchell Square
Atlanta 30303
404-688-4636

Hawaii

Thomas Hale Hamilton Library
General Reference
University of Hawaii
2550 The Mall
Honolulu 96822
808-948-7214

The Hawaiian Foundation Resource Room
130 Merchant Street
Bancorp Tower, Suite 901
Honolulu 96813
808-538-4540

Idaho

Caldwell Public Library
1010 Dearborn Street
Caldwell 83605
208-459-3242

Illinois

Belleville Public Library
121 East Washington Street
Belleville 62220
618-234-0441

DuPage Township
300 Briarcliff Road
Bolingbrook 60439
312-759-1317

Louisiana

East Baton Rouge Parish Library
Centroplex Library
120 St. Louis Street
Baton Rouge 70821
504-389-4960

New Orleans Public Library
Business and Science Division
219 Loyola Avenue
New Orleans 70140
504-596-2583

Shreve Memorial Library
424 Texas Street
Shreveport 71101
318-226-5894

Maine

University of Southern Maine
Office of Sponsored Research
96 Falmouth Street
Portland 04103
207-780-4411

Maryland

Enoch Pratt Free Library
Social Science and History Department
400 Cathedral Street
Baltimore 21201
301-396-5320

Massachusetts

Associated Grantmakers of
  Massachusetts
294 Washington Street
Suite 501
Boston 02108
617-426-2608

Boston Public Library
Copley Square
Boston 02117
617-536-5400

Walpole Public Library
Common Street
Walpole 02081
617-668-5497 ext. 340

Western Massachusetts Funding
  Resource Center
Campaign for Human Development
Chancery Annex
73 Chestnut Street
Springfield 01103
413-732-3175 ext. 67

Grants Resource Center
Worcester Public Library
Salem Square
Worcester 01608
617-799-1655

Michigan

Alpena County Library
211 North First Avenue
Alpena 49707
517-356-6188

Minnesota

Duluth Public Library
520 Superior Street
Duluth 55802
218-723-3802

Southwest State University Library
Marshall 56258
507-537-7278

Minneapolis Public Library
Sociology Department
300 Nicollet Mall
Minneapolis 55401
612-372-6555

Rochester Public Library
Broadway at First Street, SE
Rochester 55901
507-285-8002

Saint Paul Public Library
90 West Fourth Street
Saint Paul 55102
612-292-6311

Mississippi

Jackson Metropolitan Library
301 North State Street
Jackson 39201
601-944-1120

Missouri

Clearinghouse for Midcontinent
  Foundations
P.O. Box 22680
Univ. of Missouri, Kansas City
Law School, Suite 1-300
52nd Street and Oak
Kansas City 64113
816-276-1176

Kansas City Public Library
311 East 12th Street
Kansas City 64106
816-221-2685

Washoe County Library
301 South Center Street
Reno 89505
702-785-4190

New Hampshire

The New Hampshire Charitable Fund
One South Street
Concord 03301
603-225-6641

Littleton Public Library
109 Main Street
Littleton 03561
603-444-5741

New Jersey

Cumberland County Library
800 E. Commerce Street
Bridgeton 08302
609-455-0080

The Support Center
17 Academy Street, Suite 1101
Newark 07102
201-643-5774

County College of Morris
Masten Learning Resource Center
Route 10 and Center Grove Rd.
Randolph 07869
201-361-5000 ext. 470

New Jersey State Library
Governmental Reference
185 West State Street
Trenton 08625
609-292-6220

New Mexico

Albuquerque Community Foundation
6400 Uptown Boulevard N.E.
Suite 500-W
Albuquerque 87110
505-883-6240

SUNY/College at Old Westbury Library
223 Store Hill Road
Old Westbury 11568
516-876-3156

Plattsburgh Public Library
Adult Services Department
15 Oak Street
Plattsburgh 12901
518-563-0921

Adriance Memorial Library
93 Market Street
Poughkeepsie 12601
914-485-3445

Queens Borough Public Library
89-11 Merrick Boulevard
Jamaica 11432
718-990-0700

Rochester Public Library
Business and Social Services Division
115 South Avenue
Rochester 14604
716-428-7328

Staten Island Council on the Arts
One Edgewater Plaza Rm. 311
Staten Island 10305
718-447-4485

Onondaga County Public Library
335 Montgomery Street
Syracuse 13202
315-473-4493

White Plains Public Library
100 Martine Avenue
White Plains 10601
914-682-4488

Suffolk Cooperative Library System
627 North Sunrise Service Road
Bellport 11713
516-286-1600

University of Michigan-Ann Arbor
Reference Department
209 Hatcher Graduate Library
Ann Arbor 48109-1205
313-764-1149

Henry Ford Centennial Library
16301 Michigan Avenue
Dearborn 48126
313-943-2337

Purdy Library
Wayne State University
Detroit 48202
313-577-4040

Michigan State University Libraries
Reference Library
East Lansing 48824
517-353-9184

Farmington Community Library
32737 West 12 Mile Road
Farmington Hills 48018
313-553-0300

University of Michigan – Flint Library
Reference Department
Flint 48503
313-762-3408

Grand Rapids Public Library
Sociology and Education Dept.
Library Plaza
Grand Rapids 49502
616-456-4411

Michigan Technological University
Library
Highway U.S. 41
Houghton 49931
906-487-2507

Metropolitan Association for
 Philanthropy, Inc.
5585 Pershing Avenue
Suite 150
St. Louis 63112
314-361-3900

Springfield-Greene County Library
397 East Central Street
Springfield 65801
417-866-4636

Montana

Eastern Montana College Library
Reference Department
1500 N. 30th Street
Billings 59101-0298
406-657-2262

Montana State Library
Reference Department
1515 E. 6th Avenue
Helena 59620
406-444-3004

Nebraska

University of Nebraska, Lincoln
106 Love Library
Lincoln 68588-0410
402-472-2526

W. Dale Clark Library
Social Sciences Department
215 South 15th Street
Omaha 68102
402-444-4826

Nevada

Las Vegas-Clark County Library District
1401 East Flamingo Road
Las Vegas 89119
702-733-7810

New Mexico State Library
325 Don Gaspar Street
Santa Fe 87503
505-827-3824

New York

New York State Library
Cultural Education Center
Humanities Section
Empire State Plaza
Albany 12230
518-474-7645

Bronx Reference Center
New York Public Library
2556 Bainbridge Avenue
Bronx 10458
212-220-6575

Brooklyn in Touch
101 Willoughby Street
Room 1508
Brooklyn 11201
718-237-9300

Buffalo and Erie County Public Library
Lafayette Square
Buffalo 14203
716-856-7525

Huntington Public Library
338 Main Street
Huntington 11743
516-427-5165

Levittown Public Library
Reference Department
One Bluegrass Lane
Levittown 11756
516-731-5728

The Foundation Center**
79 Fifth Avenue
New York 10003
212-620-4230

North Carolina

The Duke Endowment
200 S. Tryon Street, Ste. 1100
Charlotte 28202
704-376-0291

Durham County Library
300 N. Roxboro Street
Durham 27701
919-683-2626

North Carolina State Library
109 East Jones Street
Raleigh 27611
919-733-3270

The Winston-Salem Foundation
229 First Union National Bank Building
Winston-Salem 27101
919-725-2382

North Dakota

Western Dakota Grants Resource Center
Bismarck Junior College Library
Bismarck 58501
701-224-5450

The Library
North Dakota State University
Fargo 58105
701-237-8876

Ohio

Public Library of Cincinnati and
 Hamilton County
Education Department
800 Vine Street
Cincinnati 45202
513-369-6940

The Free Library of Philadelphia
Logan Square
Philadelphia 19103
215-686-5423

Hillman Library
University of Pittsburgh
Pittsburgh 15260
412-624-4423

Economic Development Council of Northeastern Pennsylvania
1151 Oak Street
Pittston 18640
717-655-5581

James V. Brown Library
12 E. 4th Street
Williamsport 17701
717-326-0536

Rhode Island

Providence Public Library
Reference Department
150 Empire Street
Providence 02903
401-521-7722

South Carolina

Charleston County Public Library
404 King Street
Charleston 29403
803-723-1645

South Carolina State Library
Reader Services Department
1500 Senate Street
Columbia 29201
803-734-8666

South Dakota

South Dakota State Library
State Library Building
800 North Illinois Street
Pierre 57501
605-773-3131

The Foundation Center*
Kent H. Smith Library
1442 Hanna Building
1422 Euclid Avenue
Cleveland 44115
216-861-1933

The Public Library of Columbus and Franklin County
Main Library
96 S. Grant Avenue
Columbus 43215
614-222-7180

Dayton and Montgomery County Public Library
Grants Information Center
215 E. Third Street
Dayton 45402-2103
513-227-9500 ext. 211

Toledo-Lucas County Public Library
Social Service Department
325 Michigan Street
Toledo 43624
419-255-7055 ext. 221

Ohio University-Zanesville
Community Education and Development
1425 Newark Road
Zanesville 43701
614-453-0762

Stark County District Library
715 Market Avenue North
Canton 44702-1080
216-452-0665

Oklahoma

Oklahoma City University Library
NW 23rd at North Blackwelder
Oklahoma City 73106
405-521-5072

El Paso Community Foundation
El Paso National Bank Building
Suite 1616
El Paso 79901
915-533-4020

Funding Information Center
Texas Christian University Library
Ft. Worth 76129
817-921-7664

Houston Public Library
Bibliographic & Information Center
500 McKinney Avenue
Houston 77002
713-236-1313

Lubbock Area Foundation
502 Commerce Bank Building
Lubbock 79401
806-762-8061

Funding Information Library
507 Brooklyn
San Antonio 78215
512-227-4333

Dallas Public Library
Grants Information Service
1515 Young Street
Dallas 75201
214-670-1487

Pan American University
Learning Resource Center
1201 W. University Drive
Edinburg 78539
512-381-3304

Utah

Salt Lake City Public Library
Business and Science Department
209 East Fifth South
Salt Lake City 84111
801-363-5733

Wisconsin

Marquette University Memorial Library
1415 West Wisconsin Avenue
Milwaukee 53233
414-224-1515

University of Wisconsin – Madison
Memorial Library
728 State Street
Madison 53706
608-262-3647

Wyoming

Laramie County Community College Library
1400 East College Drive
Cheyenne 82007
307-634-5853

Australia

Victorian Community Foundation
94 Queen Street
Melbourne Vic 3000
607-5922

Canada

Canadian Center for Philanthropy
3080 Yonge Street
Suite 4080
Toronto, Ontario M4N3N1
416-484-4118

England

Charities Aid Foundation
18 Doughty Street
London W1N 2 PL
01-831-7798

Tulsa City–County Library System
400 Civic Center
Tulsa 74103
918-592-7944

Oregon

Library Association of Portland
Government Documents Room
801 S.W. Tenth Avenue
Portland 97205
503-223-7201

Oregon State Library
State Library Building
Salem 97310
503-378-4274

Pennsylvania

Northampton County Area Community College
Learning Resources Center
3835 Green Pond Road
Bethlehem 18017
215-865-5358

Erie County Public Library
3 South Perry Square
Erie 16501
814-452-2333 ext. 54

Dauphin County Library System
Central Library
101 Walnut Street
Harrisburg 17101
717-234-4961

Lancaster County Public Library
125 North Duke Street
Lancaster 17602
717-394-2651

Sioux Falls Area Foundation
404 Boyce Greeley Building
321 South Phillips Avenue
Sioux Falls 57102-0781
605-336-7055

Tennessee

Knoxville–Knox County Public Library
500 West Church Avenue
Knoxville 37902
615-523-0781

Memphis Shelby County Public Library
1850 Peabody Avenue
Memphis 38104
901-725-8876

Public Library of Nashville and Davidson County
8th Avenue, North and Union Street
Nashville 37203
615-244-4700

Texas

Amarillo Area Foundation
1000 Polk
P.O. Box 25569
Amarillo 79105
806-376-4521

The Hogg Foundation for Mental Health
The University of Texas
Austin 78712
512-471-5041

Corpus Christi State University Library
6300 Ocean Drive
Corpus Christi 78412
512-991-6810

Vermont

State of Vermont Department of Libraries
References Services Unit
111 State Street
Montpelier 05602
802-828-3261

Virginia

Grants Resources Collection
Hampton Public Library
4207 Victoria Blvd.
Hampton 23669
804-727-6234

Richmond Public Library
Business, Science, & Technology Department
101 East Franklin Street
Richmond 23219
804-780-8223

Washington

Seattle Public Library
1000 Fourth Avenue
Seattle 98104
206-625-4881

Spokane Public Library
Funding Information Center
West 906 Main Avenue
Spokane 99201
509-838-3364

West Virginia

Kanawha County Public Library
123 Capital Street
Charleston 25301
304-343-4646

Japan

Foundation Center Library of Japan
Elements Shinjuku Bldg. 3F
2-1-14 Shinjuku, Shinjuku-ku Tokyo
03-350-1857

Mexico

Biblioteca Benjamin Franklin
Londres 16
Mexico City 6, D.F.
525-591-0244

Puerto Rico

Universidad Del Sagrado Corazon
M.M.T. Guevarra Library
Correo Calle Loiza
Santurce 00914
809-728-1515 ext. 357

Virgin Islands

College of the Virgin Islands Library
Saint Thomas
U.S. Virgin Islands 00801
809-774-9200 ext. 487

*Regional collections operated by The Foundation Center
**National collections operated by The Foundation Center

Appendix A **Example of child care service organizational chart**

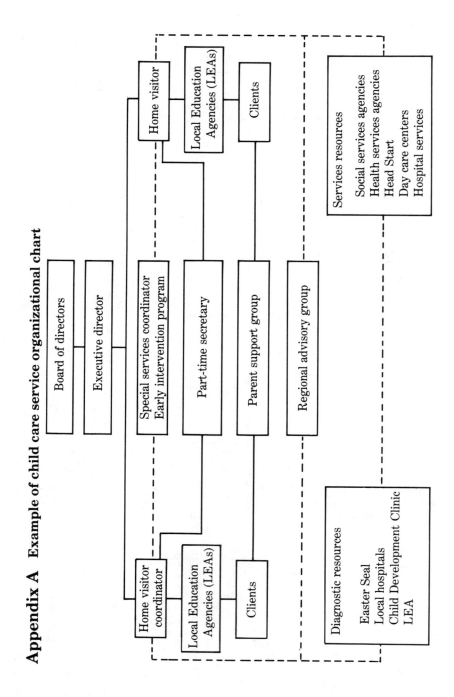

- Board of directors
- Executive director
- Special services coordinator / Early intervention program
- Part-time secretary
- Parent support group
- Regional advisory group
- Home visitor
- Local Education Agencies (LEAs)
- Clients
- Home visitor coordinator
- Local Education Agencies (LEAs)
- Clients

Services resources

Social services agencies
Health services agencies
Head Start
Day care centers
Hospital services

Diagnostic resources

Easter Seal
Local hospitals
Child Development Clinic
LEA

Appendix B

Example of statement of goals and objectives

These are *excerpts* from a proposal for the development of a home-based program for handicapped infants from birth to three years of age. The proposal was submitted for state funding by an educational agency identified here for purposes of anonymity as Riverside.

V. Goals and objectives

The Home Visitors Program is proposed as an effort to supplement Local Education Agencies' (LEAs') required identification and evaluation of infants and toddlers who are handicapped. The ultimate goal of the Home Visitors Program is to involve parents in continuing evaluation and educational planning process for their child. The home visitors will provide parent instruction in such activities as infant stimulation and will help parents identify how to best meet their child's unique needs. Because the handicapped infant is part of the family unit, efforts will be made to involve other members, such as siblings or grandmothers, in the program.

VI. Objectives, interventions, and evaluation

Riverside's Home Visitors Program has the following eight objectives:

Objective I—To promote public awareness of the birth-to-age-three identification program and Educational Service Center (ESC) services delivery model as part of an effort to locate handicapped children.

I.1 The home visitor will familiarize the medical community (obstetricians, pediatricians, hospitals, clinics, public health agencies) with the program.

I.2 The staff will familiarize LEA personnel with the program as an aid to early identification of handicapped children from birth to age three.

I.3. The staff, whenever possible, will assist the state Child Find awareness campaign for children from birth to age three by promoting a relevant public awareness campaign in both the urban and rural sections of the Riverside catchment area.

I.4. The staff will use public service announcements to promote public awareness.

Evaluation—A systematic logging of all awareness activities noting times, places, and personal contacts will be maintained.

Objective II—To log and coordinate existing assessment facilities and services available in the Riverside region for children from birth to age three.

II.1. A Regional Advisory Committee composed of parents, representatives from local agencies, LEAs, and Riverside will be established.

II.2. The staff will work with Advisory Committee in investigating such areas as: populations served by existing agencies; types of assessment available in existing agencies; populations not being assessed; areas where cooperative efforts can and cannot take place; particular training needs; cost-effective assessment centers; alerting area pediatricians to Child Find Medical Model; identification of resource person within each agency for referral purposes.

II.3. A portion of Riverside's Special Education Resource Center would be devoted to resource compilation, agency services, reading lists, literature pertinent to birth-to-age-three population. Materials would be made available to parents and professionals on a loan basis.

Evaluation—A mechanism will be devised by the Advisory Committee to monitor the coordination effort.

Objective III—To assist LEA personnel in channeling assessment requests and in receiving direct services through the home visitors program.

III.1. Riverside will contact LEA staff regarding appropriate assessment facilities in the catchment area and to inform them of the home visitor program.

III.2. Members of Riverside's diagnostic team will be available to assist in assessment when requested by LEA (clinical psychologist, occupational therapist, physical therapist).

III.3. LEA requests for home services program shall be submitted in writing to Riverside. The request shall include:

a. Pertinent information about the child. b. Signature of superintendent/supervisor. c. Copy of Individualized Education Plan (IEP). d. Parent signature.

III.4. Riverside's home visitor staff will review the requests and draft a preliminary plan regarding the extent of services required.

Evaluation—Riverside staff will document all referral assistance and home visitor programming.

Objective IV—To work closely with LEA personnel and parents in formulating plans for home intervention.

IV.1. Following Planning and Placement Team (PPT) decisions and IEP formulating by the LEA and parents, the home visitor staff will work with the LEA in scheduling an initial home visit to explain the program to parents.

IV.2. The home visitor staff will meet with the parents to outline home intervention procedures and will be available for consultation and information.

Evaluation—Parents will be provided with an evaluation form concerning initial intervention.

Objective V—To provide regular home visits and home instruction that involves the family and the child.

V.1. The home visitor will schedule weekly visits with the family to demonstrate individual program planning.

V.2. The home visitor will demonstrate for the parents methods of recording the child's progress.

V.3. The home visitor will aid the parents in devising weekly lesson plans for the child.

V.4. The home visitor will make time available during the visit for answering parents' specific questions and/or requests.

V.5. All materials and supplies will be provided by the home visitor staff.

Evaluation—-The home visitor team will keep records of all home visits and program planning efforts.

Objective VI—To encourage the development of, and participation in, parent support groups.

VI.1. The home visitor will encourage monthly meetings for the parents in order that the parents receive support from one another.

VI.2. The home visitor will act as a resource for the parent support group whenever possible.

VI.3. The home visitor will work with the parents to find a suitable location (i.e., Riverside, parents' home) for the parent support group.

VI.4. The program will receive assistance from the Riverside staff psychologist when appropriate.

Evaluation—A record of attendance and participation will be kept with each meeting, including a record of interest in the group (those who offer their home, plan events, etc.).

Objective VII—To work closely with LEAs in reporting case progress, evaluating individual programs, and program assistance.

VII.1. The home visitor team will submit progress reports to the LEAs every three months.

VII.2. The home visitor team will be available to meet the LEAs at periodic progress meetings on individual cases.

VII.3. The home visitor team will be available to LEA personnel to provide program assistance in developing comparable services in their own district.

Evaluation—Forms will be provided to LEAs for evaluation of home programming and program assistance.

Objective VIII—To provide LEAs and other agencies' staff members with training in appropriate home delivery programs for children from birth to age three and their families.

VIII.1. The staff will develop training activities to instruct LEA and agency personnel in home intervention techniques appropriate for parents and children from birth to age three.

VIII.2. The staff will develop workshops to facilitate training.

VIII.3. Consultants will be hired to provide more specific instruction.

Evaluation—Number of persons training as well as programs developed and implemented will be recorded.

Appendix C

Samples of objectives stated according to activities, responsibilities, and timelines

Objective I: To promote public awareness of the birth-to-age-three identification program and Educational Service Center (ESC) services delivery model as part of an effort to locate handicapped children.

Step #	Action plan	Person(s) responsible	Sept.	Oct.	Nov.	Dec.	Jan.	Feb.	Mar.	Apr.	May	June	July	Aug.
1	Familiarize medical community with program	Project coordinator Home visitors												
2	Familiarize Local Education Agencies with program	Project coordinator Home visitors												
3	Assist state Child Find awareness campaign in region	Project coordinator Home visitors												
4	Use public service announcements	Project coordinator Home visitors												

(Appendix C cont. on p. 67)

Objective II: To log and coordinate existing assessment facilities and services available in the Riverside region for children from birth to age three.

Step #	Action plan	Person(s) responsible	Sept.	Oct.	Nov.	Dec.	Jan.	Feb.	Mar.	Apr.	May	June	July	Aug.
1	Form a Regional Advisory Committee	Riverside Executive Personnel Local Education Agencies	——											
2	Develop a log system for recording information	Regional Advisory Committee Home visitors Staff			——									
3	Delineate areas to be reviewed and logged	Regional Advisory Committee Home visitors Staff						—						
4	Contact and alert area agencies to early identification effort	Regional Advisory Committee Home visitors Staff	—————————											

. . .

Appendix D

Standards for charitable solicitations

Developed by the Philanthropic Advisory Service of the Council of Better Business Bureaus, Inc.

Introduction

The Council of Better Business Bureaus promulgates these standards to promote ethical practices by philanthropic organizations. The Council of Better Business Bureaus believes that adherence to these standards by soliciting organizations will inspire public confidence, further the growth of public participation in philanthropy, and advance the objectives of responsible private initiative and self-regulation.

Both the public and soliciting organizations will benefit from voluntary disclosure of an organization's activities, finances, fund raising practices, and governance—information that donors and prospective donors will reasonably wish to consider.

These standards apply to publicly soliciting organizations that are tax exempt under section 501(c)(3) of the Internal Revenue Code, and to other organizations conducting charitable solicitations.

While the Council of Better Business Bureaus and its member Better Business Bureaus generally do not report on schools, colleges, or churches soliciting within their congregations, they encourage all soliciting organizations to adhere to these standards.

These standards were developed with professional and technical assistance from representatives of soliciting organizations, professional fund raising firms and associations, the accounting profession, corporate contributions officers, regulatory agencies, and the Better Business Bureau system. The Council of Better Business Bureaus is solely responsible for the contents of these standards.

For the purposes of these standards:

1. "Charitable solicitation" (or "solicitation") is any direct or indirect request for money, property, credit, volunteer service or other thing of

value, to be given now or on a deferred basis, on the representation that it will be used for charitable, educational, religious, benevolent, patriotic, civic, or other philanthropic purposes. Solicitations include invitations to voting membership and appeals to voting members when a contribution is a principal requirement for membership.

2. "Soliciting organization" (or "organization") is any corporation, trust, group, partnership or individual engaged in a charitable solicitation; a "solicitor" is anyone engaged in a charitable solicitation.

3. The "public" includes individuals, groups, associations, corporations, foundations, institutions, and/or government agencies.

4. "Fund raising" includes a charitable solicitation; the activities, representations and materials which are an integral part of the planning, creation, production and communication of the solicitation; and the collection of the money, property, or other thing of value requested. Fund raising includes but is not limited to donor acquisition and renewal, development, fund or resource development, member or membership development, and contract or grant procurement.

Public Accountability

1. Soliciting organizations shall provide on request an annual report.

The annual report, an annually-updated written account, shall present the organization's purposes; descriptions of overall programs, activities and accomplishments; eligibility to receive deductible contributions; information about the governing body and structure; and information about financial activities and financial position.

2. Soliciting organizations shall provide on request complete annual financial statements.

The financial statements shall present the overall financial activities and financial position of the organization, shall be prepared in accordance with generally accepted accounting principles and reporting practices, and shall include the author's or treasurer's report, notes, and any supplementary schedules. When total annual income exceeds $100,000, the financial statements shall be audited in accordance with generally accepted auditing standards.

3. Soliciting organizations' financial statements shall present adequate information to serve as a basis for informed decisions.

Information needed as a basis for informed decisions generally includes but is not limited to: a) significant categories of contributions and other income; b) expenses reported in categories corresponding to the descriptions of major programs and activities contained in the annual report, solicitations, and other informational materials; c) a detailed schedule of expenses by natural classification (e.g., salaries, employee benefits, occupancy, postage, etc.) presenting the natural expenses incurred for each major program and supporting activity; d) accurate presentation of all fund raising and administrative costs; and e) when a significant activity combines fund raising and one or more other purposes (e.g., door-to-door canvassing combining fund raising and social advocacy, or television broadcasts combining fund raising and religious ministry, or a direct mail campaign combining fund raising and public education), the financial statements shall specify the total cost of the multi-purpose activity and the basis for allocating its costs.

4. Organizations receiving a substantial portion of their income through the fund raising activities of controlled or affiliated entities shall provide on request an accounting of all income received by and fund raising costs incurred by such entities.

Such entities include committees, branches or chapters which are controlled by or affiliated with the benefiting organization, and for which a primary activity is raising funds to support the programs of the benefiting organization.

Use of Funds

1. A reasonable percentage of total income from all sources shall be applied to programs and activities directly related to the purposes for which the organization exists.

2. A reasonable percentage of public contributions shall be applied to the programs and activities described in solicitations, in accordance with donor expectations.

3. Fund raising costs shall be reasonable.

4. Total fund raising and administrative costs shall be reasonable.

Reasonable use of funds requires that a) at least 50% of total income from all sources be spent on programs and activities directly related to the organization's purposes; b) at least 50% of public contributions be spent on the programs and activities described in solicitations, in accordance with donor expectations; c) fund raising costs not exceed 35% of related contributions; and d) total fund raising and administrative costs not exceed 50% of total income.

An organization which does not meet one or more of these percentage limitations may provide evidence to demonstrate that its use of funds is reasonable. The higher fund raising and administrative costs of a newly created organization, donor restrictions on the use of funds, exceptional bequests, a stigma associated with a cause, and environmental or political events beyond an organization's control are among the factors which may result in costs that are reasonable although they do not meet these percentage limitations.

5. Soliciting organizations shall substantiate on request their application of funds, in accordance with donor expectations, to the programs and activities described in solicitations.

6. Soliciting organizations shall establish and exercise adequate controls over disbursements.

Solicitations and Informational Materials

1. Solicitations and informational materials, distributed by any means, shall be accurate, truthful and not misleading, both in whole and in part.

2. Soliciting organizations shall substantiate on request that solicitations and informational materials, distributed by any means, are accurate, truthful and not misleading, in whole and in part.

3. Solicitations shall include a clear description of the programs and activities for which funds are requested.

Solicitations which describe an issue, problem, need or event, but which do not clearly describe the programs or activities for which funds are requested will not meet this standard. Solicitations in which time or space restrictions apply shall identify a source from which written information is available.

4. Direct contact solicitations, including personal and telephone appeals, shall identify a) the solicitor and his/her relationship to the benefiting organization, b) the benefiting organization or cause and c) the programs and activities for which funds are requested.

5. Solicitations in conjunction with the sale of goods, services or admissions shall identify at the point of solicitation a) the benefiting organization, b) a source from which written information is available and c) the actual or anticipated portion of the sales or admission price to benefit the charitable organization or cause.

Fund Raising Practices

1. Soliciting organizations shall establish and exercise controls over fund raising activities conducted for their benefit by staff, volunteers, consultants, contractors, and controlled or affiliated entities, including commitment to writing of all fund raising contracts and agreements.

2. Soliciting organizations shall establish and exercise adequate controls over contributions.

3. Soliciting organizations shall honor donor requests for confidentiality and shall not publicize the identity of donors without prior written permission.

Donor requests for confidentiality include but are not limited to requests that one's name not be used, exchanged, rented or sold.

4. Fund raising shall be conducted without excessive pressure.

Excessive pressure in fund raising includes but is not limited to solicitations in the guise of invoices; harassment; intimidation or coercion, such as threats of public disclosure or economic retaliation; failure to inform recipients of unordered items that they are under no obligation to pay for or return them; and strongly emotional appeals which distort the organization's activities or beneficiaries.

Governance

1. Soliciting organizations shall have an adequate governing structure.

Soliciting organizations shall have and operate in accordance with governing instruments (charter, articles of incorporation, bylaws, etc.) which set forth the organization's basic goals and purposes, and which define the organizational structure. The governing instruments shall define the body having final responsibility for and authority over the organization's policies and programs (including authority to amend the governing instruments), as well as any subordinate bodies to which specific responsibilities may be delegated.

An organization's governing structure shall be inadequate if any policy-making decisions of the governing body (board) or committee of board members having interim policy-making authority (executive committee) are made by fewer than three persons.

2. Soliciting organizations shall have an active governing body.

An active governing body (board) exercises responsibility in establishing policies, retaining qualified executive leadership, and overseeing that leadership.

An active board meets formally at least three times annually, with meetings evenly spaced over the course of the year, and with a majority of the members in attendance (in person or by proxy) on average.

Because the public reasonably expects board members to participate personally in policy decisions, the governing body is not active, and a roster of board members may be misleading, if a majority of the board members attend no formal board meetings in person over the course of a year.

If the full board meets only once annually, there shall be at least two additional, evenly spaced meetings during the year of an executive committee of board members having interim policy-making authority, with a majority of its members present in person, on average.

3. Soliciting organizations shall have an independent governing body.

Organizations whose directly and/or indirectly compensated board members constitute more than one-fifth (20%) of the total voting membership of the board or of the executive committee will not meet this standard. (The ordained clergy of a publicly soliciting church, who serve as members of the church's policy-making governing body, are excepted from this 20% limitation, although they may be salaried by or receive support or sustenance from the church.)

Organizations engaged in transactions in which board members have material conflicting interests resulting from any relationship or business affiliation will not meet this standard.

Reprinted with the permission of the Council of Better Business Bureaus. Copyright © January 1982.